**Music Library Assoc^...^**
**Basic M^...^**

Jean Morrow

1. *Music Classification Systems,* b ^...^ ^...^u by Linda Barnhart, 2002.
2. *Binding and Care of Printed Music,* by Alice Carli, 2003.
3. *Music Library Instruction,* by Gregg S. Geary, Laura M. Snyder, and Kathleen A. Abromeit, edited by Deborah Campana, 2004.
4. *Library Acquisition of Music,* by R. Michael Fling, edited by Peter Munstedt, 2004.
5. *Audio and Video Equipment Basics for Libraries,* by Jim Farrington, 2006.

# Audio and Video Equipment Basics for Libraries

Jim Farrington

*Music Library Association*
*Basic Manuals, No. 5*

The Scarecrow Press, Inc.
Lanham, Maryland • Toronto • Oxford
and
Music Library Association, Inc.
2006

# SCARECROW PRESS, INC.

Published in the United States of America
by Scarecrow Press, Inc.
A wholly owned subsidary of
The Rowman & Littlefield Publishing Group, Inc.
4501 Forbes Boulevard, Suite 200, Lanham, Maryland 20706
www.scarecrowpress.com

PO Box 317
Oxford
OX2 9RU, UK

British Library Cataloguing in Publication Information Available

**Library of Congress Cataloging-in-Publication Data**
Farrington, Jim.
  Audio and video equipment basics for libraries / Jim Farrington.
     p. cm. -- (Music Library Association basic manual series ; no. 5)
  Includes bibliographical references and index.
  ISBN-13: 978-0-8108-5716-2 (pbk. : alk. paper)
  ISBN-10: 0-8108-5716-2 (pbk. : alk. paper)
  1. Audio-visual equipment--Handbooks, manuals, etc. 2. Video recordings--
Equipment and supplies--Handbooks, manuals, etc. 3. Sound--Recording and
reproducing--Equipment and supplies--Handbooks, manuals, etc. 4. Digital
video--Handbooks, manuals, etc. 5. Music libraries--Equipment and supplies--
Handbooks, manuals, etc. 6. Sound recording libraries--Equipment and
supplies--Handbooks, manuals, etc. I. Title. II. Series.

TK7881.4.F37 2006
621.389'7--dc22                                                      2005029437

# CONTENTS

---

In the 14 months between when I was first approached about writing this book and when I actually began committing words to computer, people's thoughts shifted about audio playback in libraries. Indeed, even during the intervening months from beginning this project until the end, things changed enough that I sometimes had to revise statements I wrote only weeks earlier. More and more libraries, especially academic, are going to streamed audio playback for applications such as course reserves. Access to several digital audio libraries is now available for lease, which was certainly not the case in 2002. Indeed, the whole notion of a room dedicated to audio playback is being rethought. In March 2001, Allie Goudy, music librarian at Western Illinois, asked on the Music Library Association listserve for advice on purchasing new audio equipment. Brad Short, music librarian at Washington University in St. Louis, responded that a significant expenditure on new equipment should probably be eschewed because less and less listening will be done in the library and technology is always changing. These topics will be explored in this book.

Certainly the science of audio and video playback has not stopped progressing. In consumer electronics, the dominance of two-channel audio is giving way to multi-channel sound fully integrated with video. Even while I was writing, new technologies were marketed and some withdrawn, and features that were only on the most expensive pieces of equipment became de rigueur on cheap, budget-line gear as well.

What I hope to cover in this book are the options that libraries have for delivering audio to their users, and what equipment is necessary to accomplish these tasks. This book should function as a buyer's guide, without necessarily comparing brands or models. I will also discuss maintaining the equipment. Further, this book is mainly concerned with audio and video playback for users, not recording technology for studios or audio preservation projects. Most of these applications already have audio engineers on staff (or should) who have their own biases regarding equipment.

One thing on which I will not spend much time is the matter of specifications, or numbers. It would do me little good to recommend to you that you look for amplifiers, for example, with a maximum of X% THD (Total Harmonic Distortion). The reasons are fourfold. First, testing is done under a variety of conditions, and what a manufacturer might get and publish for some figure might be different if the testing were done independently. Second, specs by themselves never tell you how an individual piece of equipment is going to sound, either by itself or in comparison to another piece. Third, there are many more important unmeasured things to consider, for example the ratio of metal to plastic construction. And finally, in the price range that most libraries buy equipment, specs generally are not as good as what one will find at the professional—or even better consumer—level.

I would like to thank several people who made this possible. My editors, Peter Munstedt and Jean Morrow, helped guide me through the process and gave me invaluable feedback on early drafts. Gary Galo, audio engineer and teacher at my alma mater, SUNY Potsdam, and now good friend in the Association for Recorded Sound Collections, also saw a draft and made several astute technical corrections. George Blood and Rudy Chalupa of Safe Sound Archive provided a great deal of technical information about their customized wiring and electrical systems. Several other colleagues involved in the audio and video industries either made suggestions about particular issues or, long before I began this book, fostered an appreciation for fine audio. Gary DeFranco did two of the diagrams in this book. I would like to thank my boss, Dan Zager, for letting me stay at home and write for extended stretches of time, and my other colleagues at the Sibley Music Library for picking up my slack. I want to thank John Mahoney and his Interlibrary Loan staff at Sibley for finding and obtaining for me some of the obscure literature I requested. My wife, Annette, read and made valuable comments on a late draft of this text; my son, Richard, allowed me many extended hours on the home computer, and for their continued support of this project I will always be grateful.

Jim Farrington
Mach 2005

# CHAPTER 1

# THE LISTENING ENVIRONMENT

Traditionally, there have been two options for libraries to deliver audio to their public: either the user has physical control over the disc or tape, or the library has staff dedicated to playing the recording for the user. There is a continuum of variation between these two models. Most typically the user has control over the item being played. This manual will also cover a third option that has become increasingly popular: taking advantage of computers and high-speed networking to "stream" an audio signal to the user.

## The Listening Room

One of the most common scenarios for audio playback in libraries has been the traditional listening room. A number of individual carrels or tables will have various pieces of audio equipment installed (almost always with a set of headphones, either permanently attached to the equipment or available for checkout at a circulation point), and the user is allowed to handle the physical item and play it as many times as wanted. A variation on this—or sometimes in addition—is to have one or more listening rooms that small groups can use to listen to or view media. In these instances loudspeakers are often used in the rooms instead of headphones.

While both of these models have served libraries for years, some librarians see them becoming anachronistic, especially in academic libraries. More and more users come to libraries with the expectation for digital online and on-demand access to all kinds of material, including sound and video. The combination of the rapid drop in the cost of computer memory together with high-speed and high-bandwidth intranet wiring have made streaming media a real possibility for libraries that did not exist even in the mid-1990s. There are still significant costs associated with the initial creation of audio files and server setup, but storing and delivering the files are relatively easy.

Nevertheless, most libraries have substantial investments in audio and video artifacts such as CDs, LPs, and DVDs that still need to be made available to people who come to the library. The advantages to traditional listening rooms include:

- **Modest staffing requirements.** Staff time is primarily needed for equipment maintenance, and checking material out to users if the recordings are closed shelf.
- **User convenience.** The listener/viewer has complete control over starting and stopping and the number of times the item is played.
- **Sound quality.** The quality of the audio signal is typically better than sound delivered over long distances (as in the staff playback model discussed below) or almost any kind of streaming service.

The disadvantages include:

- **Conservation.** Concern for the well-being of the physical object of the sound recording is minimal. This is more of an issue perhaps with LPs and tapes than with CDs, though digital discs are not impervious to mistreatment.
- **Space.** Listening rooms take up considerable library real estate.
- **Flexibility.** Listening rooms are relatively inflexible. A room devoted just to listening typically does not serve more than this one function, and once several large carrels or tables are in place they tend not to move.
- **User convenience.** Listeners must visit the library.
- **Cost.** Several hundred dollars, or more, of equipment is tied up in each carrel or listening station, plus maintenance costs.

## Listening Room and Carrel Needs

One of the keys to a successfully designed dedicated listening room is flexibility, both in the room itself and the furniture inside. Libraries being built or refurbished today are now fitted with conduits for network cabling. This certainly was not the case 15 years ago or more; those facilities constructed before the mid-1990s typically show their age and limitations now as institutions try to network every possible corner of their buildings. In some instances these kinds of wiring issues are being lessened by the increased use of wireless technology. Nevertheless, today it is inconceivable to have "too much" networking and associated infrastructure.

Lighting is another crucial component. Direct overhead lighting is good for seeing what is on the work surface, but is probably the harshest from an aesthetic standpoint. Additionally, direct lighting will detract from any video viewing in that room. Indirect lighting will be more subdued, but may require additional lighting at each workplace. Soundproofing may or may not be an important consideration if headphones are employed. Certainly it is desirable, if possible, to at least have a closed door to the room's entrance as a certain amount of extra noise will be generated by headphones played at very loud levels, or by users who sing, moan, groan, hum, or whistle along.

When carrels are used, thought should be given to their flexibility as well. Custom-made carrels constructed to the exact dimensions of existing equipment can look spectacular when initially installed and can provide excellent security. However, when equipment is changed the library must try to find units the same size (not very easy unless it is professional-grade, rack-mounted equipment) or find a way to alter the carrel to the new equipment. Modifying the carrel will either cost a great deal of money to retain its aesthetics, or else will never look as good again (which may be inevitable).

The nature of audio equipment makes carrel selection difficult. For example, turntables usually have a hinged lid that requires a significant amount of vertical space over that piece. This often relegates the turntable to the tabletop of the carrel, reducing the amount of usable desk space. Acoustically this is a less than ideal spot as well, as extraneous vibrations are more likely to be introduced (see the discussion below regarding turntable vibrations). Diminishing use of turntables in most libraries is making this perhaps less of a concern. Cassette decks are also problematic. The easiest way to ensure that they cannot be used for illegal recording is simply to remove the necessary cables going from the preamplifier to the audio input jacks. However, if the rear of the equipment is accessible it is simple enough for users to bring their own cables. The alternative is to mechanically disable recording devices, which is discussed below.

Typically, stock carrels from library catalogs are less than ideal for installing audio components. Most are too small to accommodate the combination of scores and books and equipment that patrons use simultaneously. Further, the electrical requirements for between two and five pieces of equipment (plus lighting) are much more than what carrels are characteristically designed to supply. Jack Westra has written some well-considered requirements for the space and physical requirements for listening carrels.[1]

Power and networking requirements are more intensive in a listening room than typically found in a reading or stack area. Special consideration should be given to the electrical requirements of such a space. Each workspace will demand a minimum of two AC outlets, and more likely four to six (plus one more if individual lights will be provided at each place).

It is important to try to keep the AC power cords of components away from signal cables going between pieces of equipment (particularly phono leads) in order to avoid inducing 60 Hz hum into the audio signal. Equally important, care should be given to the quality of the electricity that equipment receives when building a new space or renovating an existing room. If you have ever turned up the volume of an audio component and heard hums, snaps, and crackles, it is more likely a result of poor grounding and electrical work than a faulty piece of equipment. This kind of electrical noise degrades audio and video signals. The National Electrical Manufacturers Association (NEMA) wrote in their standard, *Application Guide for Isolated Ground Wiring Devices*, that: "The building grounding system can serve as a giant antenna and conductor of electrical noise. Noise, or electromagnetic interference, is caused by numerous transient ground currents which produce random electrical signals in the grounding system."[2]

Better wiring and building methods can minimize or eliminate such problems. The goal should be increased conductivity of the electricity while eliminating unwanted radio frequency and electromagnetic interference (RFI and EMI). NEMA notes that "reduction of these signals can provide a corresponding reduction in the possibility of incorrect commands or faulty readouts from the internal operation of the equipment. This can result in the benefits of improved equipment performance, improved accuracy, and reduced downtime."[3] The use of AC line conditioners (separate pieces of equipment into which source components, amplifiers, etc. are plugged) will be discussed below under accessories.

Proper grounding is the other key to a better electrical system. Audio, video, and computer equipment is sensitive to electrical fluctuations (as noted above), which means that each receptacle (the female electrical fitting) must have its own ground return. This can be facilitated in two ways. First, the receptacles should be "hospital grade." Superior to standard receptacles are those made by Hubbell (or their subsidiary, Bryant) or Leviton, leading manufacturers of electrical supplies.[4] Not only do hospital grade receptacles grip plugs more securely and improve conductivity, but the ground connection is isolated from the mounting strap. Those ground connections should then be brought back to an isolated bus (a conductor that collects and distributes electric currents) at the breaker panel. To complete the scheme, the bus connects to the bonded entrance ground via an additional conductor, separate from the regular neutral and ground.[5]

Minimally, the wiring from circuit to any receptacle into which equipment will be connected should be heavy gauge—10 AWG NM/B—and the receptacles hospital grade, rated at 20 amps. Better wiring would be to use MC (Metal Clad) cable, which includes an insulated ground wire. The result, in combination with a grounding scheme such as described above, is a continuous non-current-carrying shield surrounding the current-carrying conductors. Using any metallic conduit that permits the use of an isolated ground conductor will give similar results. Non-audio infrastructure loads, such as HVAC systems, should have their own "service," meaning that the electricity that supplies their power should be physically separate from the electricity being supplied to audio equipment. The electrical requirements and draw of such equipment, especially that with a motor, are very different from that of audio, video, and computers, and will affect negatively the quality of the electricity coming into the audio chain. Further, desktop personal computers generally run warmer than most audio equipment. As a result, PCs tax HVAC systems more than does audio equipment. This should be accounted for when renovating rooms to include several computers.

The Sibley Music Library at the Eastman School of Music, as an example, was opened in 1989 and exhibits two of the problems noted above. A 1300-square-foot listening room houses 43 audio and video carrels. None of the carrels were installed with network wiring, something unthinkable today. In 1999 the library explored the possibility of networking each carrel individually. Without extant conduit, it was estimated to have cost $22,000.[6]

Installing equipment in these carrels has been equally tricky, if not as expensive. Fortunately, all new audio and video equipment went into the new Sibley library. A local cabinetmaker was hired to build the carrels to exact specifications. When the carrels were initially built, the equipment was placed behind wooden faces that had holes precisely mitered so that each piece was secure without being bolted to the carrel. Ten years later, as the equipment started to fail and be replaced, the once-elegant carrel faces now look like they were modified to accommodate smaller pieces. Further, the tops to each carrel required a special tool to take out the screws and allow access to the equipment, and equipment that was on the middle shelf required almost dismantling the entire carrel to access it. While this certainly made things secure, it was exceptionally difficult for staff to get at equipment for maintenance or replacement. Plans are currently underway to renovate that room, which will involve taking everything down to the bare walls and starting over.

## Alternatives to the Traditional Listening Room

### Portable Equipment

Bradley Short, music librarian at Washington University in St. Louis, has proposed that libraries circulate personal CD players and encourage users to bring their own players, in lieu of installing as many listening carrels. His library is following that model, and has reclaimed a great deal of space that had been devoted to little-used listening rooms for much-needed stack space. For libraries that have abandoned LPs in favor of newer technologies, or for whom non-CD playback is minimal, this model makes a lot of sense. Many libraries now circulate laptop computers within the building, and some are now doing the same with wireless PDAs. Portable audio is merely an extension of that concept; indeed laptops can be used for CD listening, as well as DVD viewing. Or a library can invest in digital music players or personal video players. A brief survey in 2004 by music librarian David Hunter, at the University of Texas at Austin, showed that few libraries were actively using such devices, but that there was interest on the part of many.[7]

The advantages to this model include:

- **Space.** No library real estate is expended for audio.
- **Money.** Personal CD players are a relatively small capital expenditure for equipment, and broken equipment is easily replaced. However, there will be more continuing costs (see chapter 6).
- **Convenience.** Listening can take place anywhere in the library, or outside if players are allowed wider circulation.

The disadvantages may include:

- **Equipment.** Although users may tend not to take advantage of most features, personal players are either very minimalist and without enough flexibility, or far too complicated to use at a glance.

- **Quality.** Most portable equipment does not provide the same audio quality of even mid-fi equipment, although headphones superior to the OEM headphones help. On the other hand, younger users seem comfortable with MP3-quality audio, which is a compromise even from CD-quality audio. The quality of the sound may not be an issue in some situations.
- **Breakdown.** Headphones are often a weak link and require continual replacement.
- **Batteries.** A constant supply of AA or AAA batteries, or constant recharging of a large cache of rechargeable batteries, may be required. However, some manufacturers have introduced personal CD players (among the most expensive) that come with rechargeable batteries and charging stand. Other personal CD players with rechargeable batteries claim 50 to 60 hours of operation on a single charge.
- **Copyright.** If users bring their own equipment on which to play recordings, or even use a library-supplied portable unit, the library loses control over patrons' ability to make their own recordings. However, much as libraries cannot control to what use photocopy machines are made, they should not be held responsible for any infringement perpetrated by an individual.
- **Security.** Portable equipment is more of a target for theft, as are the batteries that run them, so there are budgetary implications.

## Distributed Audio, Staff Playback

Another model that has been implemented by some libraries is the method of staff handling all audio playback, sending the signal from a central group of audio components to a listener in a remote carrel, sometimes referred to as "hands-off." Typically the equipment is located in a staff area (e.g., behind a circulation or reserve desk) where employees put the recordings on or in their respective players, and then the signal is routed through a switcher to the user at a listening station. Often cassettes or other recording devices are available to the user to record and repeatedly play back a particular work or section, rather than play the original artifact over again. In such cases the cassette or recording medium is secured so that it cannot be taken by the user.[8] In other installations the listener has remote control over digital media playback, and staff need only play analog sources. Equipment is located in a staff area but the listener determines which digital tracks are played without staff intervention.

This model has several strengths, first and foremost being that care and security of the audio material can be of primary importance. Since only staff handles the discs and tapes, they can be carefully trained in safe and proper handling and playback techniques. A library gives up much of the safety of its material when the general public is allowed to handle and play back recordings. This is certainly more of an issue with LPs, tapes, and other less robust, pre-digital formats, not that CDs and DVDs are impervious to abuse and wear.

In a new installation, a library might see cost savings from this model in that fewer pieces of equipment are needed. Not every listening carrel would require every piece of listening equipment for the variety of formats a library has. Those savings may be balanced out by the cost of routing and wiring from the equipment to the carrels. Indeed, lack of attention to proper wiring can wreak audio havoc. In at least one installation observed at another institution, the audio signals have "bled" from one listening station to another for years, creating an audible mélange in listeners' ears. An interesting variation on this model, proposed by David Hunter, is for staff at the circulation counter to play recordings, but instead of wiring the signal to carrels patrons would have wireless headphones that could be used anywhere in a reasonable proximity to the transmitter.[9]

The real cost to the library, though, is the ongoing expense of staff time. There must be at least one dedicated person available at all times, and at times when listening activity is at its heaviest more than one person is needed. Even if only student-wage workers are used, the hours add up quickly. While major sound archives such as the Rodgers & Hammerstein Archives of Recorded Sound at the New York Public Library for the Performing Arts or the Library of Congress Recorded Sound Reference Center use this playback system because of the special nature of their collections—and the sheer variety of audio formats that they play for users—its desirability for non-archival situations is questionable.

## Distributed Audio via Digital Network

The model that is becoming increasingly popular is that of offering users audio material via the library's digital network. Often provided in addition to some other model of audio playback, many libraries are offering portions of their audio collections to users via streamed audio. Typically for academic libraries this means course reserves, but an increasing number of institutions are digitizing special audio collections and making them available as widely as copyright restrictions allow.

Further, some companies are marketing to libraries already-digitized collections of recordings. At the 2003 Music Library Association meeting, the record label Naxos debuted a way of distributing over a network everything in their catalog. Technically it was rather straightforward: Naxos supplied a subscriber with a hard drive to be mounted in a local server, and new releases would be updated by Naxos to that hard drive via the Internet. Subscribers were charged one time for a particular title to be accessed, after which that title could be listened to ad infinitum. Since then, that model has been discontinued in favor of the more typical Internet-only access from servers maintained by Naxos. As more and more commercial entities begin selling—more accurately, leasing—electronic access to recordings, even libraries that have yet to jump into audio streaming will have to confront these new distribution models for their users. Although beyond the scope of this book, prognosticators are already contemplating the ways in which libraries will be acquiring audio material as the industry is forced to change its distribution models.

The requirements of a typical distributed digital setup are akin to remote playback, the difference being that the audio does not require ongoing staff intervention to play the sound for the user. The digital file, once prepared, is available as long as the library makes it so, and users can access it electronically as frequently as they please. The equipment requirements are conventional: a streaming server connected to the library's network, at least one staff workstation where the digital files are prepared (assuming that the library is providing content from its own collections), and computers with headphones for users. A new alternative is wireless PDAs that incorporate Web browsing and Windows Media Player, which can also be used to listen to streamed audio.

The audio requirements of the end-use computers are discussed in chapter 6, the issue of using these computers also as CD and/or DVD playback devices should be addressed. When plans are being made for this kind of listening, using computers for "double duty" is a tempting way to reduce the amount of equipment needed. However, the life span of personal computers today is only a few years at best, whereas a dedicated CD or DVD player should last perhaps twice as long, and for a fraction of the cost. Even where computers are dedicated to streamed audio (that is, they are not used for word processing, catalog searching, or perhaps are not connected to the Internet) and therefore have extended life expectancies, the computer is monetary overkill for inferior audio quality. Planning for this kind of listening facility should therefore not include using computers as the only playback devices for other digital media.

Mention should be made here of Indiana University's VARIA-TIONS project.[10] At the Cook Music Library, each CD acquired has its audio content "ripped" to a server, and is then available as an audio stream at any workstation in the library or in classrooms in the school of music. Hotlinks are made in the 856 field of the MARC biblio-graphic record to provide access. Over time they will build a digital library of tens of thousands of audio files that will not only meet their students' immediate academic needs, but also facilitate new ways of incorporating digital products into their users' research. This initiative has received substantial outside funding, and at this time no other insti-tution is implementing the same kind of comprehensive digital reposi-tory of new acquisitions.

Another significant digital project is the Library of Congress's Na-tional Audio-Visual Conservation Center presently under construction in Culpeper, Virginia. This state-of-the-art conservation and storage facility will not only digitally preserve both audio and film/video, but will provide remote playback at the Library of Congress, some 70 miles away. Unlike Variations2, the emphasis at Culpeper is on deteriorating, obsolete, and endangered material. Like Variations2, their work on strategies and metadata to package digital sound recordings for remote access will likely set standards for other libraries that eventually do this kind of work.

## Space Requirements for Listening

There are no written guidelines or standards regarding the amount of listening space that should be allotted per capita, either from library organizations like the American Library Association or Music Library Association, or from music accrediting bodies such as the National Association of Schools of Music. Even if such guidelines were in place, in reality they would not be applicable in every situation. The amount of in-house listening is determined by many factors, including:

- Circulation of material (who can borrow what, and for how long)
- Size of user population
- Intensity of study (e.g. music major or non-major, large survey courses or smaller seminars, graduate or undergraduate)
- User knowledge about the existence of listening/viewing fa-cilities

- User knowledge about the collection's contents
- Use—or anticipated use—of streamed audio for reserve, especially if available outside of the library
- Convenience (physical location, number of stations, and amount of working equipment) and hours of operation of listening/viewing facility
- Use or availability of personal audio equipment

Unfortunately, unless a new building is being designed, space for listening/viewing is usually pre-determined and may or may not be adequate. How, then, does one decide the optimal size of a listening/viewing center? By weighing the criteria above, especially taking into account how much listening outside the library is anticipated, together with Westra's guides for carrel space,[11] planners can make educated estimations for a listening center.

## Notes

1. Jack Westra, "Audio Facility Planning: Furniture, Space and Construction Requirements," in *Planning and Caring for Library Audio Facilities*, edited by James P. Cassaro, MLA Technical Report no.17 (Canton, MA: Music Library Association, 1989), 3-11.

2. *Application Guide for Isolated Ground Wiring Devices* (Rosslyn, VA: NEMA, 2002), 1.

3. Ibid.

4. Information about Hubbell products is available at <http://www.hubbell-wiring.com>, and about Bryant products at <http://www.hubbell-bryant.com>, and about Leviton at <http://www.leviton.com/>. The product number of the recommended duplex receptacles for all three manufacturers is 8300.

5. I want to thank Rudy Chalupa, the electrical engineer in Philadelphia, PA who designed the electrical infrastructure for Safe Sound Studios, for explaining in plain language the construction of this model restoration studio.

6. The library has since installed a wireless network that covers the entire library for about 1/10 the cost of wiring just the listening room.

7. David Hunter, "Summary of initial responses to I-Pod for E-Res," November 10, 2004, <MLA-L@LISTSERV.INDIANA.EDU>.

8. The listening booths at the Library of Congress, however, do not have any such recording device. Until recently users were limited to two plays only from the same recording. Now, however, a DAT is made for people who require repeated listenings (although the user does not have direct control over the tape itself), and the DAT is erased immediately after the user is done with it. I am not aware of any library that allows a user to make copies of recordings

for personal use and take them away. Even though libraries have for many years posted copyright warnings next to public photocopiers on the assumption that that releases the institution from liability, no library with which I am familiar has extended that concept to audio recordings.

9. David Hunter, "wireless headphones," October 12, 2004, <MLA-L@LISTSERV.INDIANA.EDU>.

10. The original VARIATIONS project has now been expanded in scope to form Variations2, incorporating not only sound recordings but also a wide array of digital products. A full explanation of Variations2 can be found at <http://variations2.indiana.edu/>.

11. Westra, 3-6.

# CHAPTER 2

# SOURCE COMPONENTS

## Equipment Considerations for Public Listening Areas

Whether used in individual carrels, small listening rooms, or in a seminar or public meeting room, most of the equipment needs for library users are comparable. The audio playback chain can be thought of as three parts: source components (sometimes called the "front end"), amplification (also referred to as "electronics"), and sound producers. Source components are what play the media: turntables, CD players, and so forth. Amplification includes both preamplifiers and amplifiers, and sound producers are either speakers or headphones.[1]

It would be possible, and at first perhaps tempting, for a library to purchase all-in-one systems, often referred to as "minisystems" or "microsystems." This would certainly simplify setup as typically there are no connections to make, except for speakers. While minisystems are certainly a less expensive alternative, the disadvantages usually outweigh this one factor:

- Minisystems always come with speakers and, if their application in the library will only include headphones, then the money spent on speakers and the amplification section is wasted. Moreover, most minisystems do not have a headphone jack.
- When one of the components breaks down, the entire unit must be taken out of service to be fixed or replaced.
- Minisystems almost never have auxiliary inputs, so that other equipment cannot be added.
- Minisystems are rarely made with high quality components or parts, providing not only less satisfactory listening but making premature mechanical breakdowns more likely.
- It might be difficult to find a system that has only the components desired (for example, they almost always have an AM/FM tuner).

- If cassette playback is provided, it will also record. Eliminating the record function, if that is even possible, will require opening the system up and doing some kind of interior cutting or removing of certain wires, which might negate any warranty. Minisystems are generally designed to be throwaway equipment, with no thought given to someone wanting to work on the interior, even to fix it. Many minisystems also include CD-recorders and/or MP3 recording capabilities.

Separate components are what a library will usually purchase. It is becoming increasingly difficult, however, to find components that are entirely appropriate for library usage, at least as listening rooms and the like have been conceived over the past 30 or more years. For example, most manufacturers of low-end consumer electronics assume that the typical setup will be more for home theater, rather than two-channel reproduction. Therefore, instead of a single-disc CD player, the user has a multi-disc CD or DVD changer; instead of just a cassette deck, a dual-well cassette deck with high-speed dubbing capabilities is much more common. All source components are then routed through an A/V receiver and sent to five or more surround speakers. As this becomes more the norm in consumers' lives, less and less will traditional library listening facilities be embraced by our users.

Audiophiles will argue long into the night about which part of the audio chain is the most important. Into the 1970s, conventional wisdom said that the speaker (or headphone) made the most difference to the final sound, and therefore half of one's audio budget should be spent on this component. The Scottish turntable manufacturer, Linn (more specifically, its indefatigable founder and owner, Ivor Tiefenbrun), began espousing the view that the source component was the most important part of the system. His logic followed that if the signal was not picked up properly from the LP, then what happened afterwards to the signal did not matter. The audiophile boom of the later 1970s and especially the 1980s witnessed numerous specialty audio manufacturers each touting their piece of the puzzle (from cables and wires to acoustic room treatments) as the crucial element. In reality, all of these things are important, but it is how they work in combination that marks a truly fine system. System components should be matched in terms of performance, putting equipment of the same basic level together instead of one exceptionally good piece with other pieces of much lesser quality.

But does it matter in libraries? Sadly, libraries typically do not provide high quality audio for their users. The level of equipment required is deemed too expensive, and the space required for a meaningful listening experience—which, by audiophile definition, must be via properly placed loudspeakers—is more than library designers are willing to give up. On the other side of the coin, many of the components that are deemed "high-end" audio are much too fragile—and in many cases too large—to warrant consideration in a library, even if price were no object. Our users have been conditioned not to come to the library expecting to hear high quality audio. Today, when so many of our users arrive after a steady diet of MP3 and compressed audio files, most seem unaware of just how good audio can be.

Nevertheless, by using "mid-fi" equipment instead of the least expensive components, libraries can bring a modicum of pleasure to our users' listening.[2] With that in mind, the following comments about particular pieces of equipment focus on moderately priced units, rather than the price-no-object kind. It does not make sense to discuss the musical subtleties of vacuum tube versus solid state components, or the technical issues of monoblock versus stereo amplifier design, when it seems so unlikely that a library will buy that level of equipment.[3]

Do reviews matter, and if so, where does one find reputable reviews and reviewers? For librarians, who may spend considerable time reading reviews of $30 books to decide if they are worthy of acquisition, the matter of audio equipment evaluation is even more challenging. In the audiophile heyday of the 1980s and 1990s, there were dozens of journals published that reviewed equipment. Today only a handful are still in business (some of the better ones are listed at the end of this book) and most of those give equal space to home theater and video equipment. Even so, many individual models are never reviewed given the volume of new equipment being produced by manufacturers.

There are basically two kinds of professional audio reviews.[4] "Objective" reviews are those that look solely at the measurements of a piece of equipment, verify that the specifications supplied by the manufacturer are more or less correct, outline the unit's features, and then say what a wonderful piece of equipment it is. Rarely are comparisons made to similar units, perhaps because that would imply that one is better than the other, and the reviewer rarely gives an indication of what the component sounds like. "Objective" reviews simply are not critical, often for fear of offending advertisers who generate the magazine's revenue.[5] Even less useful are the general "consumer guides," which (1) almost never include mid-fi or high quality components, and (2) do not seem to provide any useful data about sound quality. The other kind of review is "subjective." Measurements are often provided and commented on, but the value of these reviews is that they actually comment on the sound, characterizing it negatively as the reviewer sees fit.

Unfortunately for libraries, most of the subjective review journals are primarily aimed at the high end, and the majority of the equipment under consideration is of the very expensive kind.[6] However, when they do review "mid-fi" equipment that a library would consider, these reviews are usually worth reading. Most of these journals have websites, often with indexes to their reviews and sometimes online versions of their reviews, either for free or to download for a price. Between 1983 and 1994, the Music Library Association published in *Notes* an annual index to equipment reviews covering almost all of the significant review journals. Today there is no one place to go for such an index, but some of them are indexed by *The Music Index* and *International Index to Music Periodicals*.

For what should a library look as regards audio/video components for patron use? First and foremost, they should be well constructed. Libraries usually want to squeeze as much usage out of a piece of equipment as possible, so they want it bulletproof. Stephen Bradley, writing about what to look for when libraries consider purchasing CD players, states: "Try to make sure there is as much metal in the construction as possible."[7] This is good advice for almost any piece of equipment, but is becoming increasingly difficult to find. A look "under the hood" of most equipment, especially lower end products, reveals not only a predominance of plastic parts, but also that of completely integrated mechanisms and circuit boards, which make it often impossible to fix a broken part. Either the entire unit must be replaced, or at least a larger and more expensive component within the unit than what is actually at fault.

Another good rule of thumb regarding equipment is: the simpler the better. The more "bells and whistles" a component has, the more that can go wrong, both mechanically and sonically (degradation of the signal). By the same token, though, we want enough functionality so that users can do what they need to. For example, do you really need pitch control on your CD player or cassette deck? Maybe you only need one or two machines so equipped. When looking for new equipment, pay close attention to which features are available only via the remote control. This simplifies the look of the unit and is therefore a popular choice among design engineers, but forces the library either to make the remote available to users, or to limit functionality. Are the functions labeled clearly? If the user cannot sit down and immediately begin to use the unit, it is either too complicated or poorly designed or both. Better yet, are the function labels etched or silk-screened on the faceplate? The latter wear off fairly quickly in a high-use environment like a library, but it is increasingly difficult to find etched markings, and never are they found on inexpensive equipment that is primarily plastic.

Something that confuses many people when looking at audio and video equipment is the issue of measurement and specifications. Every component has something to measure: THD (Total Harmonic Distortion), sensitivity, impedance, gain, S/N (Signal-to-Noise ratio), separation, frequency response, output, dynamic range, wow and flutter, rumble, and so on. The question of which measurements are important is difficult to answer. Indeed, most of today's equipment does not measure "badly" by conventional standards. At best, such specs provide some gross idea of performance, but rarely do they provide any meaningful information on which to base purchase decisions. Perhaps the main reason not to look at such measurements is that there are few industry standards regarding *how* to measure a particular facet of sound reproduction. The figures that are in one product brochure may not be comparable with those of a competing product, unless both were measured by the same third party (for example, in an equipment review). Beyond that factor, measurements by themselves give no indication of how a particular unit will sound or of its construction quality, both of which are more important that any given number.

Where does one begin to look to purchase equipment? Library catalogs are going to be of little or no help, and even catalog sellers such as Crutchfield will sell primarily the cheaper consumer-grade equipment, or offer few model choices. Further, you have no opportunity to listen to potential equipment before you buy, and should anything go wrong you have to box and ship it. I have always recommended buying locally whenever possible. Even so, one will find a variety of choices, from stores that sell audio and video equipment next to refrigerators and other household appliances (such as Best Buy) to small boutique dealers. Searching the Yellow Pages under "Stereophonic & High Fidelity Equipment–Dealers" for businesses that sell components from NAD, Adcom, Parasound, PSB, Denon, Proceed, Rotel, and similar "mid-fi" brands will lead you to local dealers who carry the right kinds of equipment. If you are in a small town that does not have such dealers, it is worthwhile exploring the offerings in nearby cities. It is to your advantage to establish a relationship with a dealer so that they can better meet your needs, both with the purchase and service or repair as needed. This is especially true when one is purchasing large amounts of equipment at once.

# Audio Source Components

## CD Players

For almost all libraries, CD players are still the main source component
for audio.[8] In many libraries they have replaced turntables and tape
decks entirely. Prices for new players range from well under $100 to
about $10,000. Since 2002 or so, however, it has become increasingly
difficult to find single-disc, stand-alone machines of reasonable quality
under $400.[9] Most machines today are either CD recorders ("burners"),
multi-disc units, or both. While a multi-disc changer may be desirable,
most libraries will stay away from publicly accessible CD burners for
the same reason libraries disable the record function on cassette decks.

CD technology continues to have long-lasting effects.[10] The basic
design parameters—being digital, using pits or bumps to encode data
and lasers to read them, even the size of the discs—have been the
model for almost every successful subsequent consumer format since
the introduction of the CD in 1982. Even though the industry is exploring new formats in an effort to find the successor to the compact disc
(more about which below), there does not seem to be a great desire on
the part of most consumers to replace their CD collections. Further,
equipment made today to play the variety of 12 cm digital discs available is universally backwards-compatible with the CD-A standard.[11]
This is good news for libraries, for which the idea of replacing tens of
thousands of CDs with a new format would be daunting to say the least,
even though more than 20 years ago librarians started replacing LP
collections with the CD itself.

Many will recall the advertising campaign at the CD's launch that
the technology represented "Perfect Sound Forever." This implied that
what one heard from those initial players and discs could not be improved. Obviously we recognize that this was marketing in the same
vein as Edison's Tone Tests of 1915 to 1925. CD players today have
many significant advances in construction quality and audible superiority over their predecessors of the early 1980s. There are two parts of a
CD player to consider when purchasing a new machine: the trans-
port/laser mechanism and the accuracy of converting the digital signal
to an analog one (D/A conversion). Less expensive models tend to have
less robust construction. The concern, then, is their ability to keep the
disc from wobbling, which would cause a disc to be inaccurately read,
or perhaps not read at all. Life expectancy of the laser itself, once considered a concern for players expected to see a great length of service,
no longer seems to be an issue.

The question of whether one laser beam or three is better seems to be moot. For the kind of equipment typically going into libraries, the audio differences are insignificant. However, it is worth noting that a single beam mechanism is easier to design and construct, and, therefore, between two components at the same price, the single beam unit should have its design money spent elsewhere. Moreover, since the single beam pickup is simpler, it is more likely to stay aligned and functional for a longer period of time.

The quality of a unit's Digital-to-Analog Converter (or DAC) is a major determinant of the overall sound quality of a particular player. That is why audiophiles prefer to use separate D/A units, the well-heeled among them often spending several thousand dollars on this component alone. Also, some preamplifiers now come with digital connections, so that the digital signal is not converted to analog in the CD (or DVD) player, but later in the audio chain. The typical audio CD uses Pulse Code Modulation (PCM) to digitize an analog signal at a sampling frequency of 44.1 kHz (see figure 2.1) and 16-bit quantization. This means that the audio waveform is sampled 44,100 times per second and the measured value of each sample is rounded off (quantized) to a 16-bit binary number (or "word") out of 65,536 possible discreet levels. In terms of sound quality these are minimal numbers, which means that there is room for improvement (as it turns out, a lot of room).

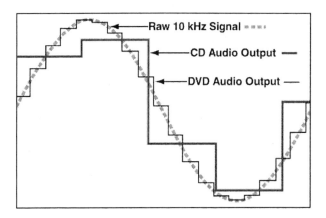

**FIGURE 2.1 Wave Signal Digitized for CD and DVD-A**

A common complaint among listeners concerning the sound of early CD players was that the upper end of the audio spectrum was not adequately reproduced. Further, it was felt that the jagged, "staircase"-like waveform was not close enough to the smooth analog signal. Figure 2.1 shows an analog sine wave (represented by dashes), and the sampling of both CD and DVD-A (DVD-Audio). The latter, while still a "stepped" approximation of the smooth analog waveform, is a much closer facsimile than the CD output. These differences are evident when listening as well. The difference between the smooth analog line, and the jagged steps is called the sampling error.

Another consideration in the conversion process is "oversampling." One way manufacturers have tried to improve CD sound quality is to sample at a higher rate than 44.1 (regardless of the word length). Oversampling provides for better audio quality than the original 44.1 kHz rate by moving some of the signal processing (quantization, or the process of converting digital to analog) out of the audible range. The high end of the audio spectrum is better, and the staircase effect is smoothed out. As a general rule of thumb, the higher the oversampling number, the better.[12]

There are two basic types of DACs: multi-bit, and single-bit. Both try to overcome the inherent limitations and difficulties of the 16-bit word length. Manufacturers have expanded the 16-bit converter to 18-, 20-, and now 24-bit converters. Other manufacturers (primarily Matsushita, JVC, and Philips, each in their own ways) have explored a simpler approach, the "1-bit" DAC, which ameliorates many of the engineering problems associated with higher bit converters.[13] Should you be concerned about these issues when making purchasing decisions? Probably not. A CD player suitable for library use is more concerned with the quality of the parts and engineering, than with what techniques are used to achieve the audible result.

There are virtually no other specification numbers that are worth considering. "Jitter" (timing faults in digital-to-analog conversion) or "clock jitter" are sometimes found in the product literature, and could potentially provide some useful comparative information. However, jitter is difficult to measure, and because there are no standards for specifying it, not all manufacturers seem to measure the same way.[14] In any event, at the price points at which libraries tend to purchase, there should not be any discernable difference.

Something else to consider when making new purchasing considerations is compatibility. Should you buy units that decode 24-bit/96 kHz discs, even though you may not yet have any in your collection? What about HDCD (High Definition Compatible Digital), which can be played by ordinary CD players, although without the special decoding that makes the HDCD a higher quality format? You could even buy DVD players, virtually all of which will also play standard CDs. Some

DVD players seem to have difficulty playing CD-Rs, which could be problematic. Using DVD players would not only let you play CDs, but also hedge your bet on the future of DVD-Audio. At this point the reader is perhaps looking for an answer to these questions. While libraries are too different to make blanket statements, it is logical to assume that most want the greatest "bang for the buck." Therefore, buying a unit that can play multiple flavors of 12 cm discs is a wise choice. There are many players today that can play DVD, DVD-A, CD, and SACD (Super Audio CD), and the prices of such players have dropped dramatically.

Another important compatibility issue regards a player's variety of output interfaces. All have a standard analog RCA stereo pair of outputs. There are a few digital audio outputs as well, some of which are better than others, and which may improve a given installation. A coaxial interface looks similar to an analog connection in that it uses a single RCA jack and is the best choice overall. The TosLink optical cable connectors (easy to recognize with their square connections) are also frequently encountered, but generally should be avoided.[15] Beyond these two common interfaces, one also finds AES/EBU, which uses an XLR connector and a balanced cable, and is the best choice when long cable runs are necessary, or, rarely, ST-Type optical.[16] All four of these connections use the S/PDIF protocol to carry digital information between pieces of equipment, but there are differences in how that is accomplished. The reason to have multiple digital outputs is simply to hedge against the future. You may not use them immediately, but it is certainly probable that future equipment connections will all be in the digital domain.

Always test any player you are considering with the kind of media you know will be used. Given that libraries do not make equipment purchases with the regularity that audiophiles or even the general public do, it makes sense to think about potential future formats (even when we do not know which ones will survive) and look at players that play new and old discs. As long as the recording industry thinks in terms of 4 ¾-inch optical discs as the medium to carry the data, backwards compatibility to CDs will be viable.

At present DVD-A and SACD are vying to become the replacement for the venerable CD. In the mid-1990s the International Steering Committee, which comprises the three major trade associations—the Recording Industry Association of America (RIAA), the International Federation of Phonographic Industry (IFPI, representing Europe), and the Recording Industry Association of Japan (RIAJ)—plus the six major international music conglomerates—BMG, EMI, PolyGram, Sony, Universal, and Warner—made a series of recommendations concerning any format that would replace the CD. Most of the requirements were aimed at anti-piracy measures and copyright protection. There was some concern with backwards compatibility with CDs, and also with audio quality, extended functionality (e.g. text, images), durability, and dimensions. Only DVD-A fully meets these requirements because SACD is an audio-only format.

Both formats have significant advantages over CDs, besides being audibly superior.[17] Of course, staying true to audio and video history, DVD-A and SACD are generally incompatible with one another, although universal players are becoming much more common, to the point that only Sony and Philips have not offered universal players.[18] At this writing, DVD-A has the disadvantage that many DVD-Video players cannot read DVD-A, although that is changing. Sometimes when audio is heard from a DVD-Video player that is not explicitly labeled as a DVD-A player, the player is not taking advantage of the DVD-A but instead reading Dolby Digital tracks that are also present on the disc.[19] The DVD Forum, the standards organization for DVD development, is developing dual-layer DVD-A (or SACD)/CD hybrid discs, which, if adopted, would eventually allow CD players to be made that would also read DVD-A and/or SACD discs.[20] Currently only SACDs are being produced in a dual-layer format. These could become important in the portable and automobile markets. To date there is a modest yet growing catalog of titles for each format, and neither has made a significant impact in the market.

Perhaps the most significant difference between CD and either SACD or DVD-A is the way the audio is coded. Whereas CD uses PCM (see above) to sample and digitize an analog signal, SACD uses an encoding method known as Direct Stream Digital (DSD), which allows for a much higher sampling frequency and greater resolution. DSD is also made necessary by the sheer amount of data that must be recorded (one second of stereo sound on a CD is about 176.4 kB, but on a SACD that is 705.6 kB, roughly four times the amount). DVD-A uses Meridian Lossless Packing (MLP, which is based on conventional PCM) for its coding.[21] Another advantage to the new formats is that they take advantage of the Reed-Solomon Product Code (RSPC) for significantly better error correction than CDs are able to provide.

One of the potential fallouts from these new formats is that they allow for multi-channel sound. Indeed, the DVD-A standard has a great deal of flexibility built in: two-, four-, five-, or six-channel mixed sound, various encode/decode choices (DTS, Dolby Digital, PCM, MLP), a variety of resolutions, as well as graphics and video features can all exist simultaneously on the same disc.[22] The DVD Forum even has a Working Group—named WG-4 and made up of more than 50 companies, but notably not Philips—to promote and develop DVD-A and the recordable DVD-AR. Late in 2004 the Fraunhofer Institute, the German research center that created the original MP3 standard, announced a new version called MP3 Surround that adds the extra audio channels without appreciably increasing file size.[23] As musicians, composers, and producers begin to take advantage of these new potentials and explore the artistic possibilities, libraries will face a dilemma: how do we provide for the faithful reproduction of such a recording, allowing our users to experience fully the intended impact?

DVD-A does raise some questions, however, that SACD avoids. Because the DVD disc can hold so much data, producers typically include a variety of coded audio, but to date many have not taken advantage of DVD-A's 192 kHz/24-bit resolution. Sonically this is the only way DVD-A can match up with SACD, which only uses this high resolution mode. Instead, DVD-A audio tracks are often 48 kHz or even 44.1 kHz (CD quality), Dolby Digital or standard PCM format. This audible crippling of the DVD-A format will not help bring consumers on board. More troubling for libraries, however, is that many DVD-As require a video monitor for setup and playback. While it may make sense, then, to purchase DVD players that can play DVD-As for the flexibility this allows, DVD-A cannot be then a stand-alone audio format.

Maintaining existing players is relatively straightforward. In fact, most of the time there is little or nothing that needs to be done. Occasionally a player will seem to cease working or have difficulty reading discs, and all that is needed is to use a laser lens cleaning disc and the unit will function normally again. If that does not fix the problem, then a technician should assess the player. The only other required maintenance is cleaning the contacts (where the cables attach to the unit) every year or two. Dirty connections between cable and any piece of equipment will diminish the sound quality over time. Torumat TC2 Contact Cleaner, now distributed by high-end cable maker Cardas, Kontak cleaner, and CAIG DeoxIT and Pro Gold can be recommended with excellent results. This is discussed in more detail later.

## LP Turntables

The playback of LPs is perhaps the trickiest part of audio reproduction. Many components, each with multiple facets, are required to take the signal as physically embedded in a record's grooves to the point where it can be converted to electrical signals and amplified to listening levels:

- The stylus—that which touches the groove of the record—comes in many different shapes.
- The cartridge comes in three varieties, moving coil, moving magnet, and moving iron, each of which can be mounted to a tonearm two different ways, standard and P-mount.
- The tonearm is available in two styles, pivoting and linear tracking (although the latter is today almost impossible to find on anything but the most expensive systems).
- Turntables have two different methods of spinning the platter, direct or belt.[24]
- A special kind of preamplifier is necessary in order to take the signal from the tonearm cartridge, boost it to the proper level, and provide the correct RIAA equalization.

The first four are interrelated, the last is more a function of amplification and will be discussed later.

The myriad engineering choices are generated by the inherent difficulty in accurate playback of a record. There are many physical forces that are at work: the rotation of the disc/platter, the force of the cartridge dragged across by the spiral of the groove (called skating),[25] the downward force of the cartridge onto the disc caused by gravity, and the three-dimensional angles (up-down, left-right, and front-back) of the stylus to the groove. Excessive force in any direction will detract from the playback of the record. Indeed, the record itself can present certain problems that make proper playback difficult, such as warpage, being pressed off-center, or being recorded at the wrong speed.

The turntable base/platter has only two jobs: to spin the record at an accurate, steady speed, and to keep unwanted vibrations from the stylus. Most turntables do a reasonable job holding a steady speed. Therefore, what marks the audible differences between turntables is their ability to keep unwanted vibrations away from the stylus/record point of contact. Since the stylus's sole function is to detect vibrations, it has no inherent way to distinguish between those that are in the groove waveform and those that come from other sources.

There are many different places from which vibrations can be generated and transferred to the disc, including the motor, the body of the turntable, and the platter. This feedback might be internal to the working of the turntable, airborne (e.g. soundwaves produced by music), or transmitted through the furniture on which it is set. Turntable manufacturers have struggled with these unwanted vibrations, going sometimes to great lengths to isolate and eliminate them by using exotic materials such as granite for the base, making super-heavy platters, or suspending the various working parts in ingenious ways, all of which can lead to turntables costing tens of thousands of dollars, plus tonearm and cartridge.

Libraries, of course, will not be buying anything so unusual. When shopping for turntables, take a moment to rap on the base with your knuckles. It should sound "dead," not hollow. The platter should be a relatively heavy aluminum. Inexpensive plastic platters or very light aluminum platters should not be considered; these are generally used only in the least expensive models where the manufacturer employs a lightweight motor that likely will not hold up under library conditions. High-tech acrylic or ceramic platters are generally beyond library means.

Regarding the two ways of making the platter spin, direct drive or belt drive, both have their advantages and disadvantages. Direct drive couples the motor to the platter. The motor turns at the speed of the record and the spindle is the motor shaft, hence the platter rests directly on the motor shaft. As long as the power supply is steady, there should be very little if any change of platter speed. Most direct drive turntables have some kind of speed control, of which the PLL (Phase Locked Loop) "servo" variety maintains an extremely accurate speed. A direct drive turntable also gets up to speed faster than a belt drive, due to the generally higher torque of the motors used. However, connecting the motor with the platter allows vibrations from the drive unit to transfer to the platter.

A belt drive turntable, where a rubber (usually) belt is wrapped around the motor and the platter, generally eliminates direct vibrations from the drive unit to the platter and is preferred by most audiophiles. However, over time (usually a long time) the belt will wear out, becoming less steady. The less expensive models of belt-driven turntables also tend to be less steady in rotational speed. There are also more parts, and therefore more parts that might need eventual repair. High-end belt drive turntables can overcome many of these problems, but that kind of engineering and manufacturing costs a lot of money.

Audiophiles spending thousands of dollars on turntables have a choice of tonearms to suit their preferences. Most of the turntables a library is likely to purchase already come with a tonearm. For better or worse, turntables currently produced that are typically in a library's price range have a pivoting tonearm. Linear tracking (LT) tonearms on budget equipment no longer exist. This is unfortunate because several years ago—into the late 1980s—Technics, Onkyo, Hitachi, and other manufacturers made turntables with this kind of tonearm that had many advantages for library use. They had a small footprint, slightly larger than an LP dustjacket, and the tonearm was incorporated into the dust-

cover. Some manufacturers made similar-sized models but with pivoting arms.

What is the advantage? A properly adjusted LT tonearm stays at a
perfect tracking angle to the grooves of the record (the way the master
record was originally cut); a pivoting arm's tracking angle is constantly
changing as it plays. Rather than being dragged along the surface of the
record by the spiral groove, a LT will be guided by mechanical means,
theoretically eliminating the pressure on the inside of the stylus. Further, a LT arm will be lighter (less mass) and shorter than a pivoting
arm. That is not to say that LT arms are without fault. Like any audio
engineering issue there are tradeoffs for both designs, and a poorly designed or implemented LT arm can negate the sonic benefits that might
have otherwise been realized. One of the main reasons that LT arms
never caught on is that the cost of designing and making a good one is
much greater than a pivoting arm.

From a library perspective, the ingenious thing about such models
is that users' hands and fingers were not needed to move the tonearm to
a different part of the disc. Simple buttons on the front of the unit accomplish that, eliminating the risk of "dragging" a cartridge across
grooves and leaving an indelible scratch. Further, since the design is
entirely mechanical there is little to do besides plugging in the cartridge, which cannot be said of maintaining accurate playing of pivoting tonearms. These kinds of turntables can still be found at auction
sites such as eBay or from stores that carry used audio gear, and often
at fairly reasonable prices. Sonically these turntables do not compare
favorably with pivoting tonearm models in the same class, but for the
reasons outlined above, they had some distinct advantages.

A pivoting tonearm is more intricate from the user's perspective.
There are more adjustments that need to be made—and kept—in order
to maintain proper playback. For the stylus to ride perfectly in the
groove, one must adjust for skating force, balance, and the position of
the stylus with regards to the groove. Skating force is the force that
drags the needle towards the center of the record, caused by the offset
geometry of the arm. If "anti-skating" is not set properly, the stylus will
exert too much force on the groove wall, not only distorting the sound
but also damaging the record. Anti-skating is also affected by the turntable being level or not. Balance keeps the stylus in the groove with the
proper amount of downward force; too much force, and the results are
obvious, but too little may be equally damaging to the record when the
tonearm is bounced out of the groove on a particularly loud passage
and it crashes down somewhere else on the disc's surface.

In an ideal world the stylus would remain perfectly in line with the
groove in the three planes: lateral, vertical, and azimuth. The Lateral

Tracking Angle (LTA, the angle of the stylus when viewed from above), and azimuth (the angle when viewed head on) are adjustments made to the cartridge as it is fixed to the headshell or tonearm. The Vertical Tracking Angle (VTA, the angle, or rake, of the stylus when viewed from the side) is often an adjustment made from the tonearm. The difficulty with VTA adjustments is that VTA—the industry standard for which is now between 20° and 25° but which began at 15°—will vary with the thicknesses of different records, and therefore can only be optimized, not made perfect. However, this particular adjustment can make a significant difference in the sound quality, especially using better cartridges. While most cartridges today are made such that when the top of the cartridge is parallel to the surface of the record the proper VTA is nominally attained, the tolerances and angles are so small that it is very difficult to be that precise. Moreover, this angle was not always the standard, and many if not most early LPs were cut at somewhat different angles. All of these adjustments are fairly straightforward, if you have the proper tools. A regular maintenance schedule should be followed to ensure not only proper sound reproduction, but also the longevity of the equipment and recordings.

Another issue that concerns pivoting tonearms but about which librarians need not be too concerned is geometry. Pivoting tonearms come in two shapes: S and straight. The theory behind the S-shaped tonearm is that it aligns the cartridge better with the groove over the course of the record and therefore produces less distortion, particularly at the end of the record. The tradeoff is that these tonearms have more mass, which is considered by many to be a sonic detriment.[26] The reality is that, among the choices librarians will make about turntables, the shape of the tonearm is not even going to be an option.

Stereo cartridges today come in two kinds of mountings—standard and P-mount—and two mechanisms to produce the electrical signal—moving magnet and moving coil.[27] The object of a cartridge is to take the physical waveform of a record groove and convert it to an electrical signal. This transformation of energy from mechanical to electrical makes the cartridge a transducer. From this point forward in the audio chain the signal is entirely electrical, until it meets the only other transducer in the audio chain, the speaker.

Despite their small size, cartridges have many components. The stylus, the part that comes into physical contact with the record, is attached to a cantilever, the tube that extends down from the bottom of the cartridge body (which holds everything together). The cantilever must be allowed to pivot in two planes—up and down, and left and right—to correspond to the modulations of the groove. These movements are transmitted to the generator, coils, and magnets, which actually convert them to electrical impulses that are sent via small wires through the tonearm and eventually into the cables that carry the signal from the turntable to their next destination. In the generator, the magnets either move within the coils and are cleverly designated Moving Magnet (MM), or the coils move around stationary magnets, which are called Moving Coil (MC). Grado cartridges, technically, are "Moving Iron" which means that there are two small pieces of iron between the magnet and the coils that move. This allows Grado to use more powerful magnets and larger coils for reduced coil inductance. For most purposes, however, they can be considered with MM cartridges because their output voltage is equivalent.

For libraries, the choice between MC (occasionally called "dynamic") and MM cartridges is easily made.[28] MC cartridges are generally much more expensive, rarely under $150. The styli are not user-replacable. Because their output voltage is significantly lower than a MM cartridge,[29] they generally require a step-up device to boost the signal to be handled by a standard phono preamplifier.[30] This step-up device, sometimes a simple transformer, but for audiophiles more likely to be an electronic device referred to as a "head amp" or "pre-preamplifier," is sometimes found built into preamps. Most preamps that are within library budgets do not have a phono stage of any kind. While Grado's moving iron cartridges do not require this step-up device, their design has a reduced coil inductance, giving them many of the positive sonic characteristics of MC cartridges.

The decision about P-mount (sometimes referred to by the designation T4P) or standard mount is driven by the kind of tonearm; they are not interchangeable. P-mount cartridges, which have four solid terminals that plug into a tonearm, tend to be much easier to install properly as there are almost no adjustments to be made. Audiophiles tend not to use P-mount cartridges for exactly that reason. They want the challenge of micro-adjusting things to get the best sound from their equipment. Libraries are better served by "plug-and-play" equipment featuring a minimal amount of setup and, consequently, a minimal amount of maintenance. There are some very good, yet inexpensive, MM P-mount cartridges made. Grado, which makes the moving iron cartridges, has a distinguished history of producing excellent equipment in all price ranges. Ortofon, Sumiko, Audio Technica, Shure, and Stanton are also well regarded.

The other factor to consider when evaluating cartridges is the shape of the stylus. Each has its plusses and minuses. Conical or spherical styli, for example, are found on the least expensive cartridges. They tend to wear out records faster due to the fact that the tracking force is concentrated on two small spots where it meets the groove wall (see figure 2.2). Conical styli do not reproduce higher frequencies well, but are considered by some to be superior for replaying particularly worn records. They are also good for 45 rpm discs and early monophonic LPs. If your playback is sophisticated enough to have turntables dedicated to specific types and eras of microgroove recordings, this is something to consider. Conical styli are also less sensitive to VTA errors.

Elliptical, or bi-radial, styli are also commonly found on less expensive cartridges. The surface area where the stylus contacts the groove wall is much greater than conical, resulting in less pressure and less record wear (figure 2.2). Thinner than conical styli, elliptical styli have superior high frequency response, and mimic more accurately the angle of the cutting stylus. Hyper-elliptical styli, or stereohedron or "shibata," extend the design for even greater surface area on the grooves and less record wear, provided they are properly installed and maintained. They are consequently more expensive, but sometimes not outrageously so. Line or linear contact—also referred to as Van den Hul, MicroRidge, or MicroLine[31]—styli are considered by many to be the best-shaped styli for retrieving the maximum of information from a record. They also tend to be found on the most expensive cartridges. A line contact cartridge on a high quality turntable/tonearm with the correct VTA can truly produce a phenomenal audio experience, one that has fueled many of the "CD-sounds-bad" battles. However, line contact and hyper-elliptical styli are more prone to VTA errors, which can actually damage records if severe enough. Elliptical styli are perhaps the best compromise for library use.

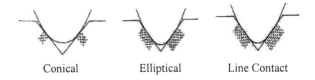

Conical          Elliptical          Line Contact

**FIGURE 2.2  Stylus Shapes. Figures from needleexpress.com.**

Occasionally one will see the term "nude" to describe a cartridge or stylus. This refers to the way in which the diamond point is affixed to the cantilever. A nude stylus has the diamond tip fitted into a hole in the cantilever, resulting in a precise and tight bond with the cantilever. The alternative, sometimes referred to as bonded, simply has the tip glued to the end of the cantilever. While less costly to manufacture, the tip is also more easily broken off, as when a user drops the tonearm onto a record. Nude styli are not typically found on cartridges within libraries' budgets.

As with most library equipment, the most important consideration when choosing cartridges is durability.[32] High-compliance, low tracking force cartridges are favored by audiophiles and high-end manufacturers, but often are equipped with cantilevers that simply do not stand up to public usage. A bent cantilever can do serious damage to a record, and may go undetected for weeks or months. In this regard Stanton cartridges are highly regarded for their ruggedness.

While all audio equipment must be periodically replaced, cartridges (more properly, styli) need replacement more regularly than electronics. An LP has about one-half mile of grooves on both sides. Taken together with the fact that the pressure at the point of contact is between 15,000 and 20,000 lbs/in$^2$ and that the temperature can reach 300°F, it becomes obvious why manufacturers recommend replacing styli after every 700-1000 hours of use. Some cartridges have replaceable styli, but with less expensive styli it may make more sense to replace the entire cartridge, especially if the library does not have access to an engineer trained to replace styli. Styli should be checked with a stylus microscope—not the naked eye—every year to gauge wear and tear. LP usage is of course declining at most libraries, and over time it will become clear how often this periodic check will need to take place.

If a library cares enough about the sound quality produced by its turntables, there are many things that can enhance even the most basic setup. Some should be considered mandatory, such as keeping the styli clean, and maintaining proper adjustments and leveling. A regular schedule for cleaning styli (based on the amount of use your turntables receive) will be rewarded by extending the useful life of both cartridge and record. Typically styli cleaners comprise a dense fiber brush to which a small amount of cleaning liquid is applied. Cleaning is *always* done in a back to front, straight line motion, or else the stylus will be knocked from its perfect angle you worked so hard to adjust. The Disc Doctor, LAST, and Discwasher all make good cleaners.[33] It should also be noted that cleaning the records themselves will make them last longer and sound better. The Keith Monks record cleaner is beyond the budgets for most libraries that do not have a sound archive, but VPI and Nitty Gritty make consumer-end record cleaners worth exploring.

Optional "tweaks" to improve performance or rectify specific problems include changing turntable mats, alternate footings, and record clamps. The typical thin, grooved, rubber mat found on inexpensive turntables has nothing to recommend it. Simply replacing the mat with something of higher quality will usually result in improved LP playback. By using a record clamp, warped records can be flattened somewhat, and already flat LPs can be held tightly to the platter, eliminating slippage. Vibrations from the surface on which the turntable sits can be reduced or eliminated by using cones or sorbothane feet. Your willingness to experiment with any or all of these enhancements may result in more pleasurable and productive listening by your users. Other modifications are mentioned in the last chapter.

The playback of earlier grooved formats such as 78s falls more in line with audio preservation and is therefore beyond the scope of this book. It is worth noting, however, that there is at least one turntable on the market that does not use a traditional stylus or cartridge. ELP manufactures a Laser Turntable that makes no physical contact made with the record grooves. At $9,900 for the base model that only plays microgroove records, the cost is not insignificant. However, the conservation benefits for a collection of recordings are a strong incentive.

**Cassette Decks**

Although never considered a high-fidelity medium, most libraries have dozens or hundreds of cassettes. Academic institutions have acquired primarily tapes that accompany books or have an archive of campus concert recordings, while public libraries have large collections of music and books on tape. For recording purposes such as reserves, cassettes have fallen out of favor in recent years in favor of CD-Rs or streamed audio. Public libraries across the country are eliminating their cassette collections, just as they have dispersed their LP collections,[34] and indeed the music industry on the whole is phasing out the cassette as a format. However, many libraries will be dealing with cassette technology for some time to come, much as LP collections are still used. This section will focus on cassette decks as playback units only, rather than their recording functions.

That the cassette should have become the dominant format in the marketplace in the last quarter of the twentieth century would have been inconceivable early in its existence. Originally intended in the 1960s as a spoken-word-only, low-fidelity medium, the development of noise reduction followed by better tape formulations, combined with the introduction of Sony's Walkman and its convenient portability, brought out the best of the cassette's attributes as a mechanism for listening to music with little dynamic range.[35]

Because virtually all cassette decks are designed for *recording*, and librarians are typically nervous about the copyright implications of that, the type of equipment that libraries would like to make available for public playback has been difficult or impossible to find. Indeed, single-well cassette decks have become almost as hard to find as single-disc CD players or affordable turntables; they are much more often found combined in one unit with a CD player or in a dual-well (that is, two-tape) configuration. Both of these configurations are designed to facilitate consumers' ability to make personal copies.[36]

A cassette deck may be the most complex piece of audio equipment a library will use. In order for the sound to be anywhere near optimal, a tape must be played back *exactly* as it was recorded, that is with the same noise reduction, bias, and angle of the tape to the head. This assumes, of course, that the tape was recorded properly in the first place. Cassette decks are much more mechanical in their construction than most audio gear, giving companies more things to market as differences between machines. There are motors, gears, solenoids, and multiple heads over which the tape passes, as well as the audio circuits for converting sound into electrical impulses and sending the signal in a recognizable format to the preamplifier. Further, the history of the medium has seen a wide variety of Noise Reduction (NR) schemes and types of tapes, which means that any cassette player must have flexibility in the kinds of tape/NR combinations that might be used.

Here is a picture of the tape path of a cassette deck, as if one were facing at an angle the "well" into which the cassette is placed.

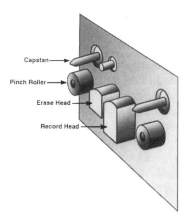

**FIGURE 2.3 Picture of Tape Path**

When the tape is inserted into the well of the deck, the pinch roller(s) raise and press the tape against the capstan(s). Better cassette decks have two capstans (and are called "dual capstan") for smoother transport of the tape. It should be noted, however, that many inexpensive "auto-reverse" cassette decks also are dual capstan, but function as single capstan since only one is functioning in each direction. In a true dual-capstan design both work simultaneously. There will be two or three heads, the erase head always being separate. The other heads are for playback and recording, but less expensive cassette decks combine these into a single head as a cost saving measure, as in this diagram. When the unit is engaged to play, the heads are raised into contact with the tape.

A three-word definition of audio tape might be "rust-covered plastic."[37] Since recording tape is a magnetic medium, metal "dust" is used to hold the signal. This metal powder was originally ferric-oxide ($Fe_2O_3$), but over the past five decades many different types of metals have been used, most popularly chromium dioxide ($CrO_2$). The metal is mixed with a "binder" that makes it stick to a thin strip of plastic, which since the 1960s has been some kind of polyester. Sometimes, but apparently not with cassette tape, the side of the tape without the metal had a "back-coating" that was to prevent print-through and secondarily to keep the tape supple over time.

Within these general parameters, however, tape manufacturers have wide latitude for creating different kinds of tapes. The International Electrotechnical Committee (IEC) established fairly broad standards for cassette recording and playback.[38] Since the standards are more general, some cassette brands work better with certain cassette deck manufacturers than others. The different types of tape not only refer to the physical makeup of the tapes, but also are indicative of what is required to correctly record or play back these tapes in the way of "bias" and equalization. A high frequency alternating current (or, bias) is introduced during the recording of a tape to reduce distortion and enhance the S/N (Signal-to-Noise) ratio.[39] Without this bias, tapes would be almost unlistenable. Each tape type requires a different amount of bias. Sonically, a tape recorded with too much bias will sound dull and muted; too little bias produces an overly bright, edgy sound. In order to properly play or record any of these tape types, your player must have some kind of switch for changing between them. This might be a manual button, or set of buttons, or the player might automatically sense the kind of tape by the type of hole in the shell.

For cassettes, there became three standard formulations, each of which uses a different bias and EQ setting: Types I, II, and IV (the original—Type 0—and Type III—ferric-chrome, or FeCr—are virtually non-existent today). Type I is ferric-oxide tape, for which the bias required is referred to as "normal" and uses 120 microsecond playback EQ. Type II, often referred to as "chrome" because the ferric-oxide particles are replaced with chromium dioxide ($CrO_2$) or an equivalent, has a higher bias and EQ (70 microsecond). Type IV, or "metal" tape, uses metallic (non-oxidized) particles to coat the tape, and has the highest record bias and 70 microsecond EQ. It should be noted that all cassette decks can *play* normal, chrome, and metal tapes, although the latter are believed to wear out heads more quickly.[40] Not all decks can *record* to Type IV tapes, however, if they lack the proper record bias. One significant impediment to proper playback of cassettes has simply been mismatched tapes and machines. Some brands or formulations of tapes play better on particular brands of cassette decks. If cassettes are going to be used extensively in some application, it could be worth experimenting to find the best match of tape and machine.

The cassette owes much of its success to Ray Dolby, founder of Dolby Laboratories, Inc. He recognized the inherent limitations of tape noise, and devised a method of compressing and expanding the audio signal on tape to greatly reduce hiss (audible random, wide-band noise not unlike the sound of air escaping a hole in a tire). All Dolby circuits work basically the same: during recording, higher frequencies are recorded more loudly than the inherent hiss of the tape, and during playback these same frequencies are played back at a much lower level to bring them back into line with the rest of the recording, which also brings the unwanted hiss to much lower levels.[41] While this sounds simple in theory, in practice the circuitry involved is very complex. Further, when tapes are played back on machines other than the one on which they were recorded, the Dolby systems in both tape decks must match both boost and cut to retain the proper frequency response.

The Dolby A Noise Reduction System, developed in 1966, had profound effects on the recording industry. These developments eventually found their way to consumer applications such as the cassette with the introduction of Dolby B, essentially a simplified version of Dolby A. Dolby B is still the standard noise reduction in use today; most domestic commercial cassettes are recorded with Dolby B, and virtually every cassette deck made in the past 20 years has incorporated this technology. There are several other noise reduction technologies that have appeared over the years, including Dolby C, Dolby SR, and dbx, as well as several proprietary—and poorly designed—knockoffs on inexpensive equipment whose manufacturers did not want to pay the Dolby licensing fees. One of the hallmarks of these competing systems, of course, is that each is incompatible with the other. That is not to say that one cannot play a Dolby C-encoded tape on a machine set to one of the other noise reduction systems, but the resulting sound will be anything but a flat frequency response. More importantly, Dolby B is the most forgiving of the various circuits regarding errors in alignment and matching level and EQ between the record and playback machines. The consumer dbx II system is particularly sensitive to differences between decks.

Besides differences in playback of a variety of tape types and noise reduction schemes, tape decks can be found with a bewildering array of mechanical possibilities or features, including different numbers of heads and motors, and options such as auto-reverse, auto-rewind, double- or high-speed or bi-directional recording, full-logic controls, pitch control, and so forth. Of these, which are important when making purchasing decisions and which are not? Motors and heads are certainly important, and pitch control may be important in some cases, but everything else is a feature.[42] That said, usually any deck that has good mechanics is also going to have a number of features that may or may not be important.

For library playback units, the most important thing to look for is a deck with two or more motors: one for the capstan(s), and one for the tape transport. Single-motor units are much less expensive to produce and more of them are made. However, multiple motors have two benefits. The one thing that most determines the quality of playback is how smoothly and evenly the tape is brought across the tape heads, and multiple-motor units are superior in this regard. Second, a single motor doing all the work is simply going to wear out more quickly than multiple motors sharing the load. Compare it to an automobile: the motor of a four-cylinder car has to work harder, and will wear out sooner, than a six- or eight-cylinder car, all other things, like weight, being equal. As mentioned above, another feature of better decks is a dual-capstan mechanism.

Occasionally one will see mention made of the kind of heads used. "Amorphous" heads are said to last significantly longer and have better dynamic range than the typical Permalloy.[43] Independent testing to verify this claim has not been found, but professional-level decks are often found with this kind of head. Ceramic heads would also be an option for extremely high use machines, or where particularly abrasive tapes are used. However, there do not appear to be any cassette decks made with ceramic heads. Since cassette decks seem to be losing more and more market share, it is unlikely that your choice for new equipment would come down to the type of head.

A discrete three-head cassette deck is only useful for recording purposes. Separating the record and playback heads allows the manufacturer to optimize each to its function, providing better frequency response and dynamic range. A single record/playback head is by definition a compromise. Three heads also allow you to monitor what the tape sounds like while you are recording it. However, for playback only units, two-head decks are perfectly adequate. One recording feature that you probably will not need is an MPX filter, which is used to enhance the quality of recording from FM radio.

Better cassette decks also have higher quality construction of the mechanisms that hold the cassette in the well. Often using ceramics or sorbothane for stabilization and insulation, the tape is held more rigidly in place, reducing vibrations (much like dampening materials used on better turntables will reduce unwanted vibrations).

Auto-reverse is a commonly found feature on cassette decks. Auto-reverse means that the tape need not be manually taken out of the deck and flipped to play the other side. The most typical implementation of this is that the tape simply reverses direction at the end, traveling at 1-7/8 ips from right to left.[44] Purists generally eschew this function, however, because it is virtually impossible for the tape going right to left to have precisely the same azimuth alignment as when it is moving left to right. Incorrect azimuth results in a muffled sound because the high end of the audio spectrum is not reproduced. Better cassette decks have used a self-correcting azimuth to ensure proper playback in both directions, but this is found primarily on the most expensive units.

# Other Audio Source Components

We have touched on the principal source components for libraries: CD players, turntables, and cassette decks. There are, of course, many other kinds of source components out there. Many of these—for example ADAT or DASH digital recording machines—are only applicable in professional recording studios. Even open reel analog recorders are virtually non-existent in most libraries. But a few other formats have made at least some impact on libraries, and there are others on the horizon that may or may not.

### MiniDisc, DAT, and MP3

Sony introduced the MiniDisc (MD) in 1992 as a digital replacement for the analog cassette.[45] Almost simultaneously, Philips (who, working *with* Sony, had produced the CD a decade earlier) introduced the Digital Compact Cassette (DCC) as an alternative. There was a time when it looked like both would fail and be a footnote under "bad audio ideas." Neither fulfilled the specifications of high quality audio. The industry, then as now, was frightened at the prospect of people's ability to make high quality digital recordings, although they recognized a consumer demand for a digital replacement for the venerable cassette. It seemed their consumer solution was to ensure poor sound quality.[46]

MDs and DCCs were aimed at consumer recording enthusiasts. Even today, there is virtually no market for pre-recorded MDs. Both formats had the ability to erase and record multiple times. The MD was certainly the more robust of the two formats. DCC's singular advantage was that it was backwards-compatible with standard analog cassettes. The cartridges were identical in size, and DCC decks could sense whether an analog or digital tape was inserted. However, like the MD, the recording did not play back with the same fidelity that people had come to expect with CDs. Both Philips and Sony used various compression schemes to keep the amount of data manageable. Compression is a digital way to delete information or data that is psycho-acoustically least likely to be missed by the ear/brain from the audio signal, thereby shrinking the file size. Their initial compression algorithms did not find favor among listeners, and indeed many audiophiles and recording preservationists today eschew any format where compression is employed.[47]

Phillips withdrew the DCC from the market months after it was introduced. Although given up for dead, somehow the MiniDisc survived, despite the fact that Sony has been almost the only manufacturer of MD equipment. One of the principal areas of the industry to embrace the MD has been radio, where MDs have largely replaced "carts" (endless cartridges used for advertisements). In 1998 Sony launched a massive advertising campaign designed to rejuvenate the format, and, as late as mid-2000, MD recorders outsold stand-alone CD-Rs and MP3 recorders.[48] Sony continues to refine and market MD technology.

And yet, the MD has never had much of an impact in most libraries. One assumes this is because libraries emphasize pre-recorded media. Some libraries have used MDs to replace cassettes for listening reserves, and for this application MDs are remarkably adequate. The advantages of indexing and track access on a disc as opposed to forwarding and rewinding a cassette make this much more attractive for reserve purposes. If cassettes are already in use for reserves, then audio fidelity is not an issue. In any event, many academic libraries seem to be moving away from any recorded media towards streamed audio for reserve listening.

MD equipment is still manufactured and sold, but only by Sony. Therefore, there is little to say in the way of purchasing MD decks. If your library uses this technology, your choices are limited. At this writing, Sony only makes one component MiniDisc unit and one combination CD/MD component, specifically designed and marketed to allow fast-speed dubbing of CDs onto MDs.[49] Most MD equipment is of the portable, Walkman style.

DAT (Digital Audio Tape) machines almost went the way of DCCs. The format was originally introduced, in 1987, prior to the MiniDisc, as a consumer format. These digital recordings did not suffer from compressed audio; recordings made digitally from a CD sounded nearly identical to the original. Executives at recording labels around the world immediately tried to put a stop to the sale of DAT machines by various means, including large taxes on equipment and blank tape. The high initial prices of DAT machines kept consumers away, but eventually the medium survived in professional studios. Before the introduction and subsequent explosion of CD-R for digital live recording, DAT was a favorite medium for many audio engineers making live recordings, including many universities and colleges across the country that record concerts and recitals. Like the MD, there is virtually no market for pre-recorded DATs.

If your library has an archive of DATs, it is likely that they are almost all live, often one-of-a-kind recordings. If this is the case, there should be in place a mechanism to transfer the data from DAT to another medium. DATs are notoriously unstable, and once a DAT tape has failed it is usually impossible to retrieve the data from it. While this book does not address in a meaningful way archiving recordings, current thinking among sound archivists regarding digital recordings points to loading data onto servers—at least two different machines and preferably more—and relying on migration and backup technology to ensure that the data is not lost. Minimally DATs should be backed up to Mitsui gold CD-Rs.

DAT seems to be a medium that will continue to be used by professionals for some time, and therefore the machines should continue to be available. As with analog cassette decks, the quality of the heads and transport assembly determines how "nice" the machine is to tapes. And as with CD players, the quality of the D/A converters largely determines how a given machine will sound. Since DAT machines are aimed at the professional (not consumer) market, their production quality is generally of a higher caliber.

Although similar in look to the cassette, DATs are mechanically much more like tapes. Therefore, cleaning DAT machines is much more difficult than cassette decks. It is wisest to take DAT machines to a professional for cleaning and alignment. Many decks include error indicators that signal the user when maintenance is required. If extreme care is not taken or the right tools not used, it is very easy to damage some of the sensitive parts, which can be very costly to fix or replace.

The mid-1990s saw the explosion of the MP3, especially among high school and college-age young adults. Since MP3 is a data file format, independent from a medium and a product of high-speed Internet connectivity, there has not been a lot to say vis-à-vis audio equipment. Indeed, by their very nature MP3s have not found a place in the audio equipment racks of consumers or professionals in the way that the formats so far discussed in this book have. Part of that is no doubt due to the poor audio quality revealed when MP3s are played on revealing equipment. Also, though, for the first time in audio history, audio content is divorced from the format storing it. Some recent CD and DVD players by Marantz, Panasonic, and others have touted their ability to play MP3 files that have been burned to CD-R/RW or DVD. Other ways MP3s are being used in libraries will be discussed below.

It seems at least conceivable now that libraries will end up using MP3 files for various kinds of playback situations (e.g. reserves). While the most ubiquitous MP3 players are either computers or portable players such as Apple's iPod or even a PDA, there are stand-alone MP3 players that can be integrated into a conventional audio system. At the time of this writing, there are few such models available.

In 2004, the newest format that seems to have potential is called DataPlay. Trying to capitalize on the portability of MP3s while coming to grips with the legalities involved, DataPlay is a proprietary new format that promises CD- or MP3-quality audio with extended playback times on a disc that is less than 1.5 in in diameter.[50] DataPlay has worked to incorporate Digital Rights Management (DRM) technology into the new format without the audible and technological problems that have plagued previous attempts. One of the intriguing possibilities of this format is that it can contain a variety of digital data: audio, images, video, documents and spreadsheets, and anything else that can be captured and stored digitally. Although it is too early to tell what the success of DataPlay will be, it is worth noting that many of the world's content providers, including EMI, Universal, and BMG, are backing DataPlay.

## Notes

1. Some audiophiles, acknowledging the symbiotic relationship between a power amplifier and the speakers it drives, identify the amplifier more in the third part of the equation rather than the middle.

2. Some favor using the cheapest equipment possible, on the assumption that (1) quality does not matter, and (2) when it breaks the equipment can be thrown away and another cheap component purchased to replace it. That model may appeal to today's throwaway society, but does nothing to help students' and patrons' listening. As will be shown in the rest of this book, there are real sonic benefits to better quality equipment, and usually the construction is more robust as well.

3. There are any number of reasons that vacuum tube equipment is impractical in libraries, even if cost is no object. Vacuum tubes need periodic replacement, thus having much higher maintenance considerations. Further, tube equipment generally runs hot to the touch (think liability), and requires

much more ventilation than solid state equipment, making it more difficult to secure.

4. Professional reviews are, of course, very different from the kind of "user reviews" that are so prevalent on the Internet, which should be used with caution if at all.

5. Two of the demagogues of objective reviewing are the late Julian Hirsch (of the now-defunct *Stereo Review*) and Howard Ferstler (who writes for *Fanfare* and *American Record Guide*, among other journals). Hirsch, like his counterpart the late Leonard Feldman who wrote for *Audio*, never heard a component that sounded less than wonderful or would write around any noticeable defects. As a result, many manufacturers clamored for his review to feed the fodder of their advertising campaigns (and were happy to support *Stereo Review* with their advertising dollars). Ferstler tries to come off as an audiophile with statements such as he "would rather listen to a great recording of a good performance than to a simply good recording of a great one" Howard Ferstler, *High Fidelity Audio/Video Systems* (Jefferson, NC: McFarland, 1991), 4. His reviews, however, show that he does not believe what his ears tell him, and that if a piece of equipment measures well then there must be nothing wrong with it. I find it unfortunate that both of these reviewers have been published in journals with such a wide circulation.

6. As Robert Harley notes, though, high-end audio does not specifically mean high-*priced* audio, although the two often go hand-in-hand. "High-end" specifically refers to audio equipment that is designed to offer a musical experience, ideally one where the recording is heard, not the equipment. Robert Harley, "What is High-End Audio?" in *The Complete Guide to High-End Audio*, 2nd ed. (Albuquerque, NM: Acapella, 1994), 1-7.

7. Stephen Bradley, "Electronic Equipment and the Music Library: An Audio Technician's Point-of-View," in *Planning and Caring for Library Audio Facilities*, edited by James P. Cassaro, MLA Technical Report no. 17 (Canton, MA: Music Library Association, 1989), 18.

8. Two relatively new digital formats are fighting it out in the marketplace: SACD (Super Audio Compact Disc) and DVD-A (DVD-Audio). Both seek to become the successor to the venerable compact disc. Should either of these—or any other high resolution audio disc format—become something libraries add to their collections and therefore need equipment, most of what is written in this book about CDs should apply.

9. One exception is the Teac CD-P1250 a modestly priced but solidly built single-play CD player with optional rack mounts. Another option are single-disc DVD players, almost all of which can also play CDs, and often a variety of other formats as well, such as SACD and/or DVD-A.

10. It is beyond the scope of this book to go into great length about how a particular format or technology works, except when it is relevant to purchasing decisions or is unusual enough to warrant some explanation. For discussions about CD technology, the reader is directed to Marshall Brain, "How CDs Work," <http://electronics.howstuffworks.com/cd.htm> (January 5, 2004); or for a more technical discussion Jan Maes and Marc Vercammen, *Digital Audio*

*Technology: A Guide to CD, MiniDisc, SACD, DVD(A), MP3 and DAT*, 4th ed. (Oxford: Focal Press, 2001), 107-31; Kenneth C. Pohlman, *Compact Disc Handbook* (Madison, WI: A-R Editions, 1992); and Ken Clements, "Compact Disc Technology," in *Audio and Hi-Fi Handbook*, rev. 3rd ed., edited by Ian R. Sinclair, (Oxford: Newnes, 2000), 67-92.

11. Not all equipment can play CD-R or CD-RW discs, which conform to a different standard than CD-A (that is, normal CD-Audio).

12. For a very technical explanation of DACs, see Maes and Vercammen, 165-73.

13. Engineers seem to have solved most or all of the problems with early ladder-type converters, however. For a good explanation of 1-bit DACs, see "Why Does It Say 1-bit Dual D/A Converter on My CD player?" <http://electronics.howstuffworks.com/question620.htm> (January 5, 2004).

14. Harley, 261.

15. To make things more confusing, there is another kind of optical cable connection, commonly found with MiniDiscs, that uses a mini-jack (a ⅛ in jack). This kind of cable is often sold alongside TosLink cables, and adaptors to go from one to the other are common.

16. ST-Type optical was developed by AT&T for the telecommunications industry. Unlike most TosLink cables, which use plastic to transmit light energy, ST-Type uses a glass-based cable, and a superior locking connector to TosLink's square plug (which many find "flimsy"). ST-Type was popular among designers of high-end audio for some time, but as engineers became more comfortable designing with the other interfaces, ST-Type has fallen out of favor.

17. Sonic superiority, however, is not the driving force for these new media. Whereas it is easy to "rip" tracks from CDs, there is as yet no tool that can do the same thing with either SACD or DVD-A. Cynics will point out that the audio industry has never introduced or promoted a format because of its audible advantages. Indeed, rarely does the highest quality format win: Edison's vertical-cut Diamond discs were sonically better than the lateral-cut records made by Victor and Columbia, and Betamax was a better video format than VHS. For more information on the development of both DVD-A and SACD, see Graham Sharpless, *New Formats for Music: DVD & SACD* (Deluxe Global Media Services, 2001–3), available at <http://www.disctronics.co.uk/downloads/tech_docs/dvdaudio.pdf>.

18. As the respective developers of SACD and DVD-A, their commercial interest lies in not promoting the other, even though both formats use the DVD disc as the physical carrier. Like the old Beta/VHS format war (and DAT/MiniDisc/DCC, and wire/tape, and 45/33 rpm, and cylinder/78 format wars before that), this will work itself out over a few years. There are now several players available that can decode both SACD and DVD-A.

19. This seems to be mostly a phenomenon with Warner/Elektra/Asylum-affiliated labels (see "Welcome to Warner Vision," n.d., <http://www.warner-vision.com.au/dvd-a.asp> [June 2, 2004]).

20. Sharpless, 3.

21. Lossless packing is analogous to using a .zip file to compress word processing documents into smaller sizes: once the file is unzipped, or in this case unpacked, every bit of data is still there.

22. Image and video playback still must handle the PAL/NTSC standards incompatibility problem (discussed in the next chapter) for proper display on a television.

23. "Audio & Multimedia MPEG Audio Layer-3," 2004, <http://www.iis.fraun-hofer.de/amm/techinf/layer3/> (November 2, 2004). Many other file formats, including Windows Media and RealAudio, are being introduced in multi-channel versions as well.

24. A third, but rarely encountered, drive system is the "rim" or "idler-wheel," which is not suitable for quality audio playback.

25. Remember the trick question in Pictionary: how many grooves does a standard record have? The answer is two, one on each side, except for Laurie Anderson's experimental record, *United States Live*, which had multiple grooves per side, and the indeterminacy of which groove the cartridge would enter was part of the meaning of the album. Some test records were also made with multiple grooves per side.

26. The overall mass of the tonearm is not as crucial as matching the cartridge mass and stylus compliance to a particular tonearm. The arm/cartridge resonance frequency should be in the 10-12 Hz region (below the level of hearing, but above that of a record warp). Therefore, higher compliance cartridges (typically MM) are suited to a lower mass tonearm, and low-compliance cartridges match better with medium-mass arms.

27. Another variety of transducer, the crystal cartridge, is no longer made. Ceramic cartridges, similar to the crystal and still occasionally found, require a much greater tracking force and should not be considered.

28. There is a third class of cartridge, ceramic piezo-electric, but their sonic characteristics are so poor as to not be worth mentioning.

29. A typical MM cartridge will have an output of 3-7 mV, a MC 0.2-2 mV. Therefore the MC cartridge needs 20-30 dB of gain to match the output of a MM.

30. Denon and Ortofon have both produced high-output MC cartridges that do not require the step-up device, but these are exceptions to the rule. In any event, the non-replaceable stylus drives up the maintenance costs over time.

31. MicroRidge is trademarked by Schure, and MicroLine by Audio Technica, but refer to the basic shape and footprint of this kind of stylus, first patented by A.J. Van den Hul.

32. However, it might be well argued that in the case of a cartridge, the most important consideration is matching it to the tonearm on which it will be mounted, followed closely by its durability.

33. Lagniappe Chemicals Ltd., P.O. Box 37066, St. Louis, MO 63141; 314-205-1388; <www.discdoc.com>. The LAST Factory, 2015 Research Drive, Livermore, CA 4550-3803; 925-449-9449; fax 925-447-0662;

<www.last-factory.com>. Recoton Corporation, 2950 Lake Emma Road, Lake Mary, FL. 32746-6240; 800-732-6866; fax 407-333-1628; <www.discwasher. com>.

LAST also makes something they call "Stylus Treatment" that "dramatically reduces the friction at the stylus/groove interface by reducing the surface free energy of the vinyl." This is supposed to further lengthen the life of the stylus and be sonically beneficial. I am aware of no testing of these claims other than LAST's own, but the data that LAST presents is very persuasive.

34. Jennifer Feehan, "Hancock Joins Library Trend, Deletes Tapes: Cassettes Being Removed to Make Room on Shelves," January 3, 2003, *The Toledo Blade* (available at <http://www.toledoblade.com/apps/pbcs.dll/article?AID= 2003101030099> [January 7, 2003]).

35. The MusiCassette was introduced by Philips in 1963. Indeed, this was as early as such an innovation might have been introduced. Prior to the early 1960s, Ampex and Jack Mullen held virtually every American patent regarding magnetic recording. The result of this was a stranglehold on development unless one wanted to pay large royalties. Once these patents began to expire, many companies began to introduce low cost equipment into the American market.

36. Interestingly, at a recent copyright workshop given by Laura Gassoway, she was of the opinion that any duplicating machine—photocopier, scanner, CD burner, tape recorder, etc.—could be made available without liability to the library as long as the necessary notices for copyright compliance were posted. However, since section 108 of Title 17 (the U.S. copyright code) only refers to printed material, this may not be applicable to audio reproduction equipment.

37. Early open reel tapes had paper as their base, but every other tape formulation, including digital tape, has had some kind of plastic as the base.

38. IEC Publication 94A.

39. Sony has introduced their 160 kHz "Super Bias" on some recent high-end machines. According to their South African website (there is no information about Super Bias at Sony.com), "To maintain distortion free recording and playback, Super Bias boosts the bias frequency to an extremely high frequency (160kHz). This effectively removes the 'beat' effect caused by high order harmonic distortion." <http://www.sony.co.za/glossary_frame.asp?Index=S> (August 11, 2004).

40. Whether or not metal tapes wear out heads more quickly is somewhat debatable. No testing has been found that verifies this claim, but there is anecdotal evidence that leads to this conclusion. In any event, the cost of Type IV tapes over the other types, combined with many listeners' complaints that Type IV sounded "duller," has meant that metal tapes have never been a large part of the market.

41. That is perhaps an oversimplified—if essentially accurate—explanation. A more complete description would note that Dolby Noise Reduction is both a dynamic and complementary system: dynamic because the amount of signal processing is dependent upon the level and frequency distri-

bution of the input signal; complementary because a process is applied during recording, and then the opposite process is applied during playback. Dolby B boosts low level information above 400 Hz during record. The lower the level, and the higher the frequency, the greater the amount of boost. In playback, the opposite takes place. Level and equalization matching between the record and playback machines is necessary for Dolby to work optimally. My thanks to Gary Galo for this clarification.

42. One feature that some users find helpful is a "memory stop," which makes the cassette stop at a particular preset number on the counter. When a short portion of music is listened to repeatedly, this is a handy feature to always return to a certain point on the tape.

43. "Amorphous" refers not to the shape of the head itself but to the alignment of the metal particles. Among these kinds of heads are ferrite (and hot-pressed ferrite) and Sendust, which are two to six times as hard as Permalloy.

44. At least two auto-reverse cassette decks did not roll the tape in the opposite direction: the Nakamichi RX-202 and RX-505 employed a "unidirectional" reverse that automatically ejected the tape, flipped it around, and reinserted the tape into the well.

45. For Sony's history of the MiniDisc, please see "MiniDisc: A Replacement for the Audio Compact Cassette," 2001, <http://www.sony.co.jp/en/Fun/SH/1-21/h4.html> (August 27, 2002). More complete information from a variety of sources can be found at *The MiniDisc Portal*, n.d., <http://www.minidisc.org/> (August 27, 2002), and Maes and Vercammen, 220-80.

46. The professional digital recording media became the Digital Audio Tape (DAT). Initially DAT prices were beyond all but high-end consumer means, another way of keeping the evils of digital recorders away from the masses.

47. Sony uses a compression scheme called ATRAC (Adaptive TRansform Acoustic Coding), and Philips one called PASC (Precision Adaptive Subband Coding). Both are "lossy" compression schemes, which means that some amount of digital information is thrown away, not reconstructed for playback. A very subjective mathematical construct, it is up to the ingenuity of the programmers whether or not the listener agrees with what information is left out and whether it detracts from the audible playback. ATRAC has gone through many versions, each one an audible improvement over the last.

48. Jon Iverson, "CD-Recorders, MiniDisc, and MP3 Running Neck, Neck, & Neck," *Stereophile*, July 10, 2000, <http://www.stereophile.com/shownews.cgi?791> (August 27, 2002).

49. To quote from Sony's advertisement of the MXD-D400, "A CD player is integrated within the MD recorder so you can transfer all of your favorite music from Compact Disc to MiniDisc," <http://www.sonystyle.com/is-bin/INTERSHOP.enfinity/eCS/Store/en//USD/SY_DisplayProductInformation-Start;sid=vRZGaT3LzKtGaX3cYohMYnLbQyHaro5RJnI=?CategoryName=hav_HiFiComponents_MiniDisc&ProductSKU=MXDD400&Dept=hav> (August 27, 2002).

50.  According to DataPlay, the disc stores 500 MB of digital data, or around 11 hours of MP3 audio files, or five hours of CD-quality audio.

# CHAPTER 3

# VIDEO

## Source Components

### Videotape

The advent of the DVD has brought audio and video closer together. DVD was originally an acronym for Digital Video Disc and later Digital Versatile Disc, belying the developer's original intent for the medium to carry more than just video. In many libraries, video playback is as important—in some cases more important—than audio. Most libraries now have at least two formats, DVD and VHS tape, and some have significant LaserDisc holdings as well. Librarians who do not maintain archival collections of video material should count their blessings if these are the only formats they must handle: there have been hundreds of formats and variations of video recorders just since the 1950s, each requiring special playback equipment that can no longer be purchased and, in some cases, serviced.

Almost all of our non-archival video collections, though, go back only as far as the mid-1970s. Sony introduced the spectacularly unsuccessful Betamax in 1975, followed the next year by JVC's VHS format. There ensued a several year format war that ultimately established the VHS as the dominant home consumer video format *despite* its poorer quality. In 1980, Pioneer began marketing the LaserDisc to the public. Although it had superior video playback qualities, the fact that it could not record kept this segment of the market fairly small.[1]

Due to its dominance in the market for more than 20 years, libraries have more VHS videotape on their shelves than any other format, and will likely need to use and maintain VHS machines for many years to come. There are many similarities between sound cassettes, particularly DATs, and videocassettes, not the least of which is the fact that the tapes themselves and the machines that play them are very complex.

The design implications that the original Ampex engineers faced when developing a way of recording video and sound to magnetic tape were formidable. One of the first problems they needed to solve was how to put such a large amount of data onto a tape. Certainly the linear recording method used for audio would not work, at least at realistic speeds.[2] The ingenious way that the designers got around this was to make the video head—actually two heads on a drum, 180° apart—rotate at 30 revolutions per second, effectively making the tape seem to move past more quickly. While this keeps tape length manageable, it increases the complexity of getting the tape through the VCR properly.[3]

As this book is being written, pre-recorded VCR tapes are on the wane. As the consumer market moves to DVD as the preferred medium for video rental, the industry produces fewer tapes, and consequently fewer manufacturers will be making units on which to play back videotapes. For libraries with significant numbers of tapes, the issues will be the same as the change from LPs to CDs. Those libraries that maintain and use their videotape collections will need to have access to good, working VCRs. Unlike LPs, though, videotape is not a videophile medium. Few will lament its passing, and at some point new equipment will cease to be made.

For what, then, should one look when purchasing what may be your last VCR? These comments assume that you are looking primarily for a playback unit, and that any recording functionality is at best incidental. Most of the generalities expressed about audio equipment apply to video as well: better-made units with higher quality parts cost more.

There are two basic kinds of analog VCRs: VHS and Super-VHS (or S-VHS).[4] The latter has significantly better video resolution (400 horizontal lines, versus about 250 for regular VHS), but requires S-VHS-encoded tapes to take advantage of it. Developed by JVC in the mid-1980s, the S-VHS was a niche-market format for a decade and a half. Its main advantage was as a recording medium, as few film studios released videos in that format. S-VHS decks are backwards-compatible: you can play a regular VHS tape on them, but you cannot play an S-VHS tape on a non-S-VHS unit. Their prices have dropped to the point where they are equivalent to a good non-S-VHS unit. The lack of commercial material, however, means that most libraries need not concern themselves with S-VHS.

Another common distinction is between Hi-Fi and standard VCRs. While the VCR has never been considered a high-fidelity audio system, Hi-Fi units are significantly better at delivering the audio portion of the videotape. At the very least the sound is delivered in stereo, while many non-Hi-Fi VCRs are only monophonic. This should be considered an essential "feature" if the VCR will be playing anything beyond the spoken word. Another important feature is the number of heads. While two heads are adequate, four-head machines are superior. Not only will the picture be sharper at a variety of speeds, when paused the picture remains clear with a four-head VCR. Six-head VCRs are mainly an advantage in situations where they will be used for a lot of recording because two heads are dedicated to recording.

Another kind of VCR that is something of a specialty unit is the "multi-system." Video standards are different in various parts of the world, and tapes made to play to one standard generally will not play accurately on another.[5] The standard in America and Japan is NTSC, but elsewhere you will find PAL, PAL-SECAM, and M-PAL. A multi-system VCR will allow you to play a PAL tape in the United States. While virtually all mainstream tapes likely to be purchased by libraries should be playable on standard VCRs, tapes imported from Europe, bought at the local ethnic market, or picked up by faculty members traveling around the world are likely not to conform to the NTSC standard. Libraries that have such tapes should probably have at least one multi-system unit. While these machines used to be very expensive and hard to find, today they are available from a number of manufacturers at much more reasonable prices.

Combination decks, units that play DVDs and play and record VHS tapes, are increasingly popular among consumers. Interestingly, unlike CD/cassette combination decks, most such video combinations are made either to not record at all from DVD to VCR, or, at the very least, not from DVDs that are Macrovision protected.[6] Virtually all of the other features one finds in advertisements concern a VCR's ability to record (e.g. VCR+, or the ability to skip commercials). Generally, in a public area the more simple the unit, the less problems one is likely to encounter. Beware that VCRs are likely to require use of the remote control unit to access some—or even most—of their features.[7] If providing security for the remotes is of concern, look for VCRs where most of their functionality can be accessed from buttons on the front of the unit.

To clean or not to clean VCRs is a question upon which experts disagree. On the one side, cleaning advocates point to the buildup of particles from tapes on VCR heads (much like on audiocassette heads), which not only diminishes picture quality but also damages both tapes and heads. Those who eschew cleaning other than by a trained technician note that there does not seem to be a cleaner available that does not do more damage to the heads than the buildup of gunk does. Some VCRs have an automatic head cleaning feature, but this seems to be more of a marketing tool than a feature that works.

## DVD

Videotape has rapidly given way to DVD. DVD has any number of advantages over VHS and LaserDisc, including superior sound and video quality, the ability to move quickly and precisely to a different part of the video, no degradation of the picture after repeated playback, a variety of viewing formats (e.g. letterbox, or sometimes different viewing angles) and subtitle options for video viewing, and compatibility with other disc formats. Another plus for libraries is that they take up significantly less shelf space.

As mentioned above, one of the possible advantages for libraries is that DVD players also play audio CDs.[8] Libraries that have limited space and/or are on a particularly strict budget can have one machine providing both audio and video. Another option some libraries consider is installing computers with DVD drives. That makes for a very expensive DVD player, unless the machine is considered for other uses as well, but results in less availability of the machine for DVD playback. There are now many DVD decks that also combine a VHS player, allowing greater flexibility from a single piece of equipment. As mentioned above, unlike dual-well cassette decks or CD/cassette combos the VHS side cannot record from the DVD, eliminating copyright infringement concerns.

The DVD format is much more technologically complex than the CD.[9] DVD and CD discs, while identical in dimensions and similar in construction and materials, are quite different. Like CDs, the data is encoded on DVDs using pits and bumps that are in a concentric spiral beginning at the inner part of the disc. In order to hold the amount of data that digital video requires, DVDs are composed of multiple layers of plastic and reflective metals, typically aluminum and gold. Further, the pits and bumps on DVDs are both smaller and significantly closer together: the bumps are 320 nm[10] (or .32 microns) wide and 120 nm (.12 microns) high, and the distance between adjacent tracks is only 740 nm (.74 microns), resulting in a track which, if lifted from the disc and straightened, would span 7.5 miles. CDs are wasteful by comparison, with 1600 nm (1.6 microns) separating tracks, and twice the minimum pit length. This also means that DVD player lasers can use a smaller wavelength than CD players, 640 nm compared to 780.

More data is put on the disc by using multiple layers of pits and bumps. By using different reflective metals (the outer layers will usually have gold, the inner aluminum) the DVD laser can be focused on different depths of the disc. Using both sides of a disc for data, and two layers per side, a DVD can store about 16 GB. A CD has only one layer of information and stores about 700 MB of data. Another difference between DVD and CD is the error correction used. CDs use a redundancy scheme, which by DVD standards is unnecessary and which limits the amount of data that can be encoded.

Digital video is further complicated by the compression format used, known as MPEG-2. Just as MP3 compression is the algorithm that determines what are the important components of an audio signal that are kept for playback, MPEG-2 (which for some reason was never shortened to "MP2") is the industry standard that compresses video into a manageable data size. Each frame is further analyzed by the MPEG encoder and determined to be one of three kinds of frames: intraframe, predicted frame, or bidirectional. Each kind of frame is compressed to a different level depending on how different it is compared to the preceding and following frame.

Fundamentally, a DVD player is quite similar to a CD player. A motor spins the disc at varying speeds depending on which part of the disc is being read. The laser that reads the pits and bumps is mounted on a tracking mechanism that must move precisely from the inner to the outer part of the disc (and back, in the case of a multi-layered disc). Keeping the laser focused in exactly the spot it needs to be on a second-by-second basis is the most difficult part. The laser reads the data as changing patterns of light reflected off of the metallic layer, and must then send that information to a DAC, or as a digital signal to another component.

Some of the differences between DVD players may not be influential in a purchasing decision for libraries. For example, the ability to decode Dolby Digital,[11] DTS (Digital Theater Systems),[12] or other surround sound is only useful if you have a proper home theater playback. Any aural advantage to this information is lost in typical two-channel (headphones or speakers) playback, although as noted in chapter 5, some headphones now seek to re-create the surround experience. Further, some DVD players output 5.1 surround expecting to be routed through a surround sound receiver that would decode the information, while other DVD players do the decoding themselves. If the library is not playing back in surround, the point is moot except insofar as paying for such a decoding feature that is not useful may seem a waste of money.

One important figure that must be compared is the specification of the audio DAC. Even some of the cheapest DVD players now come with a standard 96 kHz/24-bit DAC, which is perfectly adequate for movies. Many newer players, including some inexpensive models, have a 192 kHz/24-bit DAC, which is necessary to play DVD-Audio discs. Even if a library does not have DVD-A discs in its collection, if this format ultimately becomes popular, a library that already has DVD players with the better DAC will be ready.

As with VHS, DVD players must be able to output to your local video standard (NTSC in the United States and Japan, PAL most other places). Fortunately, even many relatively inexpensive DVD players can output both signals.[13] Besides NTSC/PAL compatibility issues, DVD players and discs are coded to certain "regions" or "zones" of the world.[14] Studios do this because movies are not released at the same time around the world: a movie just being released in theaters in the United States might already be released on video in Europe, or vice versa. Therefore, in an attempt to prevent moviegoers from avoiding the box office, and sometimes just to prevent a movie from being seen in a particular part of the world, DVDs are encrypted with a 1-byte code that tells the player where it can be seen. Some discs are coded "region-free" or "all region," meaning that any player should be able to show it. Some players can be "hacked"—either through an obtuse sequence of buttons or commands on the unit's remote, or with a special chip that is sure to void the warranty—to show discs from any region. Many Internet sites are devoted to this topic, but this is probably not a recommended practice for libraries. Computers that have DVD drives can be loaded with software that takes care of both the region issue and NTSC/PAL compatibility.

A relatively new wrinkle in DVD players is "progressive scan," which allows a direct digital connection from the DVD to a progressive or digital television, producing superior video quality from those discs that are so encoded.[15] Even if you use an analog TV as your viewing source, progressive scan DVD players usually have better picture quality, although it may not be as noticeable on the small viewing monitors libraries often employ. Some DVD players also have a feature called "enhanced black level setting" (or some similar phrase) that allows the user to change the contrast before the signal goes to the video monitor. This is an advantage in viewing areas that are brightly lit.

Another useful video feature is "3:2 pulldown" (more properly but never seen as "2:3 pulldown"), which employs a processor that compensates for the different frame rates of video and film, resulting in a better picture regardless of the source. Film (35 and 70 mm) is shot at a rate of 24 frames per second and shown on the screen at double that rate, but NTSC video is shown at nearly 30 frames per second. When film is transferred to video, some frames are repeated so that the result is not faster than intended. However, certain flaws creep into the final product, which 3:2 pulldown is designed to correct.[16]

Most DVD players have a variety of video and audio output connections. What you need will be determined by the input on whatever video unit you use to see the image (TV, computer, or monitor). All players will have a basic Video Out, a yellow jack, using RCA connectors that are usually referred to as Composite, and most players will also have an S-Video Out. The other video outs you are likely to see are Component, Optical, and Coaxial Digital. Superior connections are made with DVI (Digital Visual Interface) or HDMI (High-Definition Multimedia Interface).[17]

Composite video output provides the lowest quality (LaserDisc is composite video), but is universally accepted by almost any video unit. The S-Video Out also uses a single cable, but separates color from black and white signals and has a better resolution. Better yet is Component video, which has three cables, labeled Y, Pb, and Pr.[18] If your video monitor has three matching inputs, this yields the best analog output. When purchasing new equipment, this should be considered the minimum-grade connection.

The next step up from Component video is a digital link between the DVD player and monitor and receiver, either optical or coaxial, not to be confused with optical or coaxial digital *audio* outputs. These also require a corresponding input on the video monitor. The three most common digital video connections are RGB, Firewire (IEEE 1394, also marketed under the name i.LINK for digital audio), and DVI (and most recently DVI's likely successor, HDMI). RGB is the standard computer monitor connection, and is capable of data transmission as well as high quality video, including HDTV. Firewire is the popular interface developed by Apple for rapid transmission of data between a computer and peripheral via a serial bus. The speed with which Firewire transmits large amounts of data has encouraged some use in home theater, but most manufacturers have moved towards DVI. The advantage of these digital connections is analogous to the audio argument: the longer the signal stays in the digital domain before converting to analog, or the less time a signal spends in the analog domain, the better the result.

DVI has been the industry's answer to sending and receiving the large amount of data needed to represent that digital video combined with multi-channel digital audio. DVI incorporates the ability to transmit both analog and/or digital signals, and is based on the RGB technology used for computer flat screens, for which it was originally intended. This gives DVI the bandwidth to support even the 1080p/60 video format. DVD manufacturers have not rushed DVI-enabled players to the market yet, although more are becoming available.

The next generation of interface, HDMI, also is a high bandwidth connection that supports YCbCr component data for a better picture. Moreover, HDMI is also designed to incorporate control data between components, lessening the number of remote controls required. Fortunately HDMI is designed to be relatively backwards-compatible with DVI equipment, although the different connectors will require adapters.[19]

The "next big thing" in DVDs will be High Definition (HD) DVDs. At this writing, there are two competing HD formats. One is backed by Sony and a consortium of other consumer electronics companies (including Panasonic, Dell, Philips, and Hewlett-Packard) and is called "Blu-ray" because of the kind of laser it uses.[20] Discs can hold up to six times the data (about 50 GB), and the HD picture is said to be nothing short of stunning. The competing format, also based on blue laser technology and called HD-DVD, with the backing of NEC and Toshiba (and with help from Microsoft), is also supposed to have an excellent HD picture quality, but does not have the capacity of Blu-ray discs (30 GB). However, these discs could be made in existing DVD plants at much less cost. Although HD-DVD already has the support of the DVD Forum, the standards body for DVDs, which also includes the backers of Blu-ray, it is not at all clear which format will be released to consumers. As HDTV (more about which below) gains in market share, the drive to offer a medium that takes full advantage of the possibilities will certainly increase.

## Video Display

Not long ago the decision-making process for buying some kind of display unit for watching video programming from VHS or DVD was relatively straightforward, based largely on the amount of space one had. Until recently, one used some kind of direct-view television that occupied a lot of cubic-inch real estate. Even small televisions were deep and somewhat bulky pieces of equipment because they all used cathode ray tubes (CRTs) for showing the image. Today there are many options worth exploring, and even though the price of the latest technology is out of the range for most libraries, those numbers will eventually drop to levels that libraries can consider. However, all of these new video display possibilities create a confusing maze of options.

For libraries, space is usually as much an issue as cost, and new video options will allow libraries to make video available where it was once impossible. That makes the matrix of choices much more complex. Issues of size and shape frame the first questions to answer. Once the dimensions are considered, matters of kind of display (CRT, LCD, plasma), aspect ratio, resolution, connections, digital versus analog, HDTV, etc. all come into focus.

To determine the size screen needed for a particular installation, a simple rule-of-thumb for 4:3 ratio screens is to measure the distance in feet between the viewer's head and the front of the screen, and multiply that by 3 to 6 (in inches, measured on the diagonal across a screen's surface). Since most viewing done in a carrel is fairly close, small monitors (between 12 and 17 in) are the appropriate size. If the monitor is too small, not enough detail will show and viewers will strain their eyes; if it is too large, the viewer will not be able to take in the entire picture without moving away. However, if widescreen (16:9) displays are used, that number shrinks to roughly 1.5:2. Therefore, you can use a larger widescreen monitor for the same distance.[21]

There are basically two kinds of monitors to consider: CRT (or direct view) and LCD.[22] Direct view monitors are the traditional technology, and yet there are still advantages over some of the newer technologies. Both direct view and LCD monitors are usually easy to see in a well-lit room. The depth of "blackness" produced by a CRT is unmatched by LCD, resulting in greater contrasts between light and dark. CRTs generally display motion better than LCDs, although LCDs are getting better. Direct view monitors are the least expensive kind of monitor, especially for the screen size, as well. However, the most significant drawback is that direct view monitors take up much more surface area and are much heavier, limiting the number of places such a monitor can be installed. CRTs that have a curved screen also must be seen from closer to straight ahead, as their angle of viewing from side to side is less than that of flat screens.

LCD monitors are almost universally more expensive (for the same size viewing area) as direct view, but the price gap is narrowing.[23] Because there is no tube used,[24] LCDs can be quite thin (about 3 in) and light, allowing for much greater latitude in placement and arrangement, including wall mounting. They use very little power. LCDs are very bright and color-rich, making them suitable for viewing even in very bright rooms, and are notable for being viewable from a wider off-axis angle than direct view monitors. One source of confusion is that CRTs can be "flat screen" but still not thin like LCD panels. Flat screen direct view monitors are becoming more common, but tend to be somewhat more expensive than traditional, curved CRTs. Flat screens are much less susceptible to glare (a room's ambient light reflected back from the surface of the screen).

The next important consideration is digital or analog. Digital monitors—which can be CRT or LCD—are a relatively recent but not unexpected phenomena and they offer several advantages over their analog counterparts, especially if the source is a high quality DVD or digital satellite signal. One of the most significant reasons to consider a digital monitor is that it will accept a digital signal from the source, removing the layer of loss from which D/A conversion suffers. Eventually all televisions sold will be digital as broadcasts similarly move to digital-only.[25]

One significant advantage to digital monitors is that they can display progressive scan DVDs properly. If you already have DVD players and are looking to mate an appropriate monitor, check first what connections the DVD player offers. If the DVD offers RGB, DVI, or HDMI outputs, make sure the monitor will accept those connections to obtain the best possible picture. If none of these are present, and it is a progressive scan DVD and has a Progressive Component output, try to ensure that the monitor can accept that. A step down from Progressive Component is Progressive Interlaced, which you will likely find on DVD players that are not progressive scan. The perceivable differences between interlace and progressive displays are lessened with smaller screens, but, as screen size increases, progressive displays look comparatively better than interlaced.

One step beyond digital TV is HDTV, or Hi-Def.[26] An HDTV monitor is by definition a digital TV, but one capable of much higher resolution, and therefore superior picture quality. To see this better picture requires a high definition signal, which in turn requires a special tuner for HD programming. Many sets sold for HDTV are more accurately described as "HD-ready" or "HD-compatible" because they do not have the HD tuner built in. HD sets have, to date, been aimed at the large screen market, but this technology is filtering down to smaller sizes as well.

As this is being written, Japan's national broadcasting agency, NHK, is working on the next generation of HDTV, Ultra High Definition Video (UHDV), which boasts a mind-boggling 32 million pixels of resolution (compared to HDTV's 2 million) and a refresh rate of 60 frames per second, twice that of HDTV. If the library's video viewing does not include any kind of broadcast—that is, if only DVDs and videotapes are to be shown—then HDTV is not an issue. Moreover, both HDTV and UHDV are technologies for large screen viewing, which further limits library applicability.

HDTV programming is actually available in a variety of formats, resulting in shorthand nomenclature such as "1080p." The number refers to the lines of resolution. The following letter will either be "p" or "i," which refer to progressive or interlaced. HDTV sets often are either 1080i or 720p. The former has more lines of resolution, but the latter's progressive scan display is often felt to be more accurate, especially with fast-moving images.

The next choice to be made regards the aspect ratio. Televisions have traditionally used an aspect ratio of 4:3, which means that the screen is four units wide and three tall. This ratio was established in 1889 when one of Thomas Edison's associates was developing the ki-netoscope. This film ratio was eventually adopted by Hollywood, and, in the 1940s, carried over as the NTSC standard for broadcasting. In response to television, Hollywood movies began in the 1950s to be released in a variety of widescreen formats such as Cinemascope. Eventually theaters settled on an aspect ratio of 16:9. Although rela-tively new to home theaters and televisions, eventually all broadcasting will be done digitally in 16:9, and all televisions sold with this aspect ratio as well. At this writing the most significant downside to 16:9 screens is that most broadcasting is still done 4:3, and many older videotapes owned by libraries are altered to fit 4:3 screens. This means that the resulting picture must either be stretched to fit the screen, re-sulting in significant distortion, or the picture must be boxed in the middle to maintain the proper aspect ratios. Although widescreen moni-tors are more expensive at the moment, libraries should try to accom-modate 16:9 monitors into future budget considerations.

A monitor's resolution needs consideration only when looking at LCDs. A CRT television has a maximum of 480 lines of resolution, period. However, LCDs have several possible resolutions. Resolution refers to the number of pixels (Picture Elements) per square inch; the larger the number, the better the resolution and picture quality. One of the reasons that HDTV has so much more detail than NTSC video is that the digital pixels are less than one-quarter the size, resulting in more than four times the number of pixels per square inch.

One final thing to consider is the connections that a monitor al-lows. Minimally you should have Component Video connections be-tween your source and monitor. Planning for the future should incorpo-rate the possibility of one or more possible digital connections (Fire-wire, DVI, or HDMI as discussed above). One of the principal reasons for insisting on Component Video or better is to eliminate the need to worry about the monitor's comb filter. Comb filters serve to provide greater detail to the picture, and reduce discolorations from composite signals. However, poor comb filters, or those out of adjustment, can actually make a picture worse, possibly losing vertical resolution and inducing a halo effect around sharply contrasting objects.[27]

Comb filters come in four varieties: two-line, three-line analog (which seems to have died out in the mid-1990s), 2D three-line adap-tive, and 3D YC (or 3D motion adaptive), in ascending order of quality and price. If looking for a monitor to feed a composite single, 2D or 3D comb filters should be considered a minimum. Both types have their proponents, and neither is perfect. For example, some 3D comb filters do not work well with fast-moving images. Monitors with 3D filters tend to be much more expensive, making 2D a more attractive option.

A library might consider eschewing television sets altogether in favor of computer monitors. This is an especially attractive option when the video source will be a DVD player, and the necessary NTSC tuning for television or built-in speakers is not required.[28] The prices for such monitors are usually several hundred dollars less than for televisions with the same size and picture quality. Whether a computer monitor will or will not serve a library's needs as a video monitor will largely be based on whether it was designed to accept something other than a PC video feed. One word of caution, though: many DVI-D devices also carry the HDCP (High-Bandwidth Digital Copy Protection) protocol, and a DVD player, for example, that sends a DVI signal to a monitor will require the monitor to also be HDCP compliant.

Some may be tempted to purchase a "combo" set, that is, a single unit incorporating a monitor with a DVD and/or VCR. These can be attractive where space is very limited, or where having two or more pieces of equipment is inconvenient or impractical. They also simplify setup. However, there is a very practical reason for using separate pieces: when something breaks—and it will—one must replace not only a monitor or source component, but the entire unit, even if some part still works. Further, only a very few models have anything but a composite connection from the DVD to the monitor, eliminating any advantages of progressive scan or component connection.

Finally, once a video monitor is purchased and installed, a calibration DVD should be used to make final adjustments to the picture, and to check that the unit was not damaged or altered during shipping.

## Notes

1. LaserDisc is not discussed in this text because it is not a current format. For those libraries that have collections of LDs that need to be supported for some more years, it is worth noting that LDs came in two varieties: CAV and CLV. Needless to say, they are incompatible.

2. Video has perhaps 500 times the density of information of sound, which would require tape to move at a speed of several feet per second over a stationary head like an audiocassette uses, requiring then many miles of tape for a one- or two-hour program.

3. For a more detailed explanation of the inner workings of a VCR, see Marshall Brain, "How VCRs Work," n.d., <http://www.howstuffworks.com/vcr.htm> (May 15, 2004).

4. Digital-VHS has to this point not made a significant impact in the market. In particular there are no pre-recorded D-VHS tapes, and it is likely that this format will not last. Like S-VHS, it is backwards-compatible, but boasts better sound and audio when a D-VHS tape is used. Some Panasonic and JVC camcorders have used MiniDV cassettes, but there is almost no market for this format, which remains very expensive.

5. To be more precise, what happens is that the signal that the VCR sends to the monitor cannot be accurately displayed.

6. Macrovision is a code found on some DVDs that, when detected by a chip in the player, is supposed to block the ability to copy from DVD to VHS. Macrovision has been implemented in a number of ways by DVD player manufacturers. Depending on what kind of monitor or TV you use to view the DVD, there may be problems, especially if you are planning to use a computer's video card. If you are going directly from the DVD to a TV with Composite video outputs (the yellow jacks), there should be no problem, but this also provides the least quality of video.

As I was finishing this book, it seemed that this trend of excluding recording from one format to another in combination decks was reversing as several manufacturers were releasing decks that internally recorded DVDs to VHS, and VHS to DVD-R, but not those discs that are copy-protected.

7. Some units now made have no buttons that provide functionality, and even the most basic commands are done with the remote. It is very difficult today to find VCRs that have more than just basic playback functions as buttons on the front panel.

8. Many early DVD players have difficulty with CD-Rs because the wavelength of laser required to read DVDs is different, causing the CD-R to appear blank. Some DVD player manufacturers are adding a second laser that works with CDs and CD-R/RWs. Indeed, there are many CD variants that may or may not play on DVD players. For a complete listing see "DVD's Relationship to Other Products and Technologies," *DVD FAQ*, <http://www.dvddemystified.com/dvdfaq.html#2> (June 11, 2004). Multi-format players for both SACD and DVD-A generally can play any disc format.

9. There are actually numerous DVD standards, of which four are relatively common. DVD-5 is the basic and most common DVD, being single sided and single layered (SS-SL). DVD-9 is sometimes referred to as RSDL (Reverse Spiral Dual Layer), which effectively doubles the amount of data that can be stored by having a second track written on a different layer. DVD-5s are silver in color, DVD-9s are golden. DVD-10 has largely fallen out of favor with the introduction of DVD-9 (DS-SL), and contains a track on each side of the disc (requiring it to be flipped, like a 78 or LP). This format is still used by some manufacturers who put widescreen or letterbox video on one side, and altered-for-TV video on the other (or, more rarely, NTSC on one side and PAL on the other). Finally, the DVD-18 is both double sided and double layered (DS-DL), and gold in color on both sides. An uncommon format is DVD-14, which has two layers of data on one side (gold) and one on the flip side (silver).

10. A nanometer is one billionth of one meter.

11. Dolby Digital, released in 1991, was one of the first successful multi-channel audio systems. It employs five discrete channels: two speakers in front of the viewer (like standard stereo), two in the rear, a center speaker, plus the ability to add Low Frequency Effects (LFE) through subwoofers. This became known in shorthand as "5.1" (the subwoofer effects being the ".1") and is also known as AC-3 (Audio Code 3). Dolby, in conjunction with Lucasfilm, later added a rear center channel and introduced THX Surround EX.

12. DTS (the name of the company and the system) is a competing proprietary surround system. Backed initially by Universal, DTS made its debut in 1993 with Steven Spielberg's *Jurassic Park*. By the mid-1990s DTS had developed consumer electronics applications, and has been widely accepted by many movie studios for their video releases. DTS is now also widely used on DVD-Audio discs. There are several "flavors" of DTS. The original is 5.1, much like AC-3. When Dolby/THX released their 6.1 format (THX Surround EX, which added a center rear channel), DTS responded with DTS-ES, which itself has two versions: discrete and matrix. DTS-ES matrix requires a special chip to decode a rear channel signal that is encoded with the left and right rear signals, whereas the discrete version gives each channel its own track.

13. It should be noted, though, that some DVD players will only play NTSC, and others only PAL. Most players sold in PAL countries (that is, not the United States or Japan) will also play NTSC DVDs (although it is usually a compromised signal), but the reverse is not true. For more detailed information see "Is DVD-Video a Worldwide Standard? Does It Work with NTST, PAL, and SECAM?" *DVD FAQ*, <http://www.dvddemystified.com/dvdfaq.html#1.19> (June 11, 2004). Libraries that collect video material from around the world, or who are developing collections for local immigrant populations, may find this to be problematic.

14. There are eight codes. 1: The United States and its territories, plus Canada; 2: Japan, Europe, South Africa, and the Middle East (including Egypt); 3: Southeast Asia and East Asia (including Hong Kong); 4: Australia, New Zealand, Pacific Islands, Central America, Mexico, South America, and the Caribbean; 5: Eastern Europe (former Soviet Union), Indian subcontinent, Africa, North Korea, and Mongolia; 6: China; 7: Reserved; and 8: Special international venues such as airplanes.

15. Progressive scan was introduced by Toshiba in 1999. Most television video is "interlaced," which refers to the way the viewer displays the video frames on the screen. NTSC video is refreshed at a rate of 30 frames per second, whereas film is 24 fps. When film (or a PAL signal, which is 25 fps) is transferred to NTSC video output the image quality is adversely affected (for example, diagonal lines look jagged rather than straight). Progressive scan "de-interlaces" the signal and sends to the video screen a sequenced feed that retains the single frame clarity of film, but which requires a progressive scan input to decode. This problem is generally obviated going from film to PAL, given the close frames per second. However, since it is not an exact one-to-one ratio, there is a difference in both pitch and running time with PAL and film,

and the DVD community is setting standards to provide for progressive scan for PAL as well.

16. For a much more thorough and technical explanation of 3:2 technology, see Don Ramer, "What the Heck is 3:2 Pulldown?" 2000, <http://www.dvdfile.com/news/special_report/production_a_z/3_2_pulldown. htm> (June 17, 2004).

17. European players also have a 21-pin SCART (Syndicat des Constructeurs d'Appareils Radiorécepteurs et Téléviseurs) connector that is a combination composite and S-video.

18. Even Component video has two flavors: Component interlaced analog video (EIA 770.1) and Component progressive analog video.

19. For more information on HDMI see Alen Kobel, "HDMI—One Year Later: A New Standard for Transmitting Digital Video Signals," *Widescreen Review*, Issue 24, May 2004, available at <http://www.hdmi.org/pdf/ WSR04HDMI.pdf> (June 10, 2004). There are questions regarding how backwards-compatible the HDMI standard really is, especially since HDMI has much more to do with audio than does DVI.

20. If this format wins, readers should refrain from crying "Blu-ray for Hollywood."

21. There are many standards for calculating viewing distance and screen size, most based on the assumption that viewing will be done in a room or theater, rather than a carrel. A handy calculator can be found at <http://www.myhome-theater.homestead.com/viewingdistancecalculator. html>.

22. When considering large screen video (over 30 in, when measured on the diagonal), there are several other choices, ranging from plasma screens to various kinds of rear and front projection units. Each has its strengths and weaknesses, but is outside the scope of discussion of individual viewing.

23. The principal reason for the higher prices, besides simply cashing in on it being the latest and greatest, is the cost of manufacturing. Rejection rates for displays can reach a staggering 40%.

24. LCDs use high intensity white light from fluorescent tubes projected through cells of liquid crystal. Three such cells (one each red, green, and blue) make up each pixel. An electrical charge is applied by a matrix of thin film transistors, changing each cell's molecular structure to let through the proper amount of light. Liquid crystals were first observed in 1888, and RCA began experimenting with LCDs in 1968.

25. In 1997, the FCC mandated that all broadcasts should be digital by 2006.

26. One also encounters televisions marketed as EDTV, or Enhanced Definition TV. This is something of a poor-man's HDTV, a display that can accept HDTV signals but lacks the resolution for true HDTV. Since these are primarily plasma and other large display monitors, they fall outside this discussion.

27. For a very detailed explanation, see Allan W. Jayne, Jr., "TV Comb Filters," June 6, 2000, <http://members.aol.com/ajaynejr/vidcomb.htm> (June 10, 2004).

28. Several monitors even now are marketed for computers but have built-in tuners.

# CHAPTER 4

# ELECTRONICS

## Amplification

Many audiophiles consider amplification to be the heart and soul of the audio chain. However, in many library applications, an amplifier as a discreet component is not necessary. There are two parts to the amplification chain: the preamplifier, commonly referred to as "preamp," and the power amplifier.[1] They can be combined into one component called an "integrated amplifier." The basic function of this section of the audio chain is to raise the voltage and current of the signal sent by the source component to levels that will power a loudspeaker or headphone. A common analogy is to the power steering unit of a car: to your input (turning the steering wheel) is added torque and speed (or in the case of an amplifier, energy), which are then sent to the wheels (or, speakers).[2] This is technically more challenging than it might seem, hence the wide variety of choices and price ranges.[3]

Libraries that use listening stations with only a CD or DVD player and headphones can perhaps avoid this part of the audio chain if the player has a headphone jack. Headphones are just small speakers, and powering them properly requires a small power amplifier (an "op-amp" or "operational amplifier"). A true power amplifier, then, can be considered overkill. While this would save the cost and space of another piece of equipment, the audio quality of most headphone jacks found on disc and tape players is quite poor. Better sonic results, then, are achieved by sending the signal from the player to a headphone amp (see below). Surround sound issues are discussed under headphones.

### Preamplifiers

The preamp is the component through which source components (e.g. CD player, turntable) are routed and their signals increased on their way either to headphones, or a power amplifier and speakers. In this respect it functions more like a system's nerve center. Most importantly, the preamp controls the overall volume of the output. The output voltages for most source components are too low to be fed directly into an amplifier, hence the need for an intermediary step-up device. From a purist's standpoint, the only function of a preamp (besides switching between components) should be to increase the signal voltage to the point where an amplifier can take it and send it to speakers, not altering the signal. This is sometimes referred to as "straight wire with gain."[4] Some preamplification functions can also be built into source components, for example many CD players have a volume control and enough gain to successfully drive an amplifier. As a discreet unit in an audio system with multiple source components, the preamplifier is used by the listener to determine which source is selected for listening. This is also referred to as a control amplifier.

A preamp also may incorporate some equalization functions, minimally treble and bass adjustments, often referred to as "tone controls" and universally reviled by audiophiles, and balance between left and right channels. Passing the signal through these extra electronic components degrades the audio, even if only slightly, but such knobs seem ubiquitous on low end—and even much mid-fi—equipment. More frequently on A/V receivers but sometimes on preamps or integrated amps, one may find a DSP (Digital Signal Processor) switch. This allows the user to intentionally alter the sound to mimic being in a rock concert, concert hall, jazz club, or other venue. Some users may enjoy such possibilities, but it certainly destroys any semblance of the true sound of the recording.

There are several audio devices that are either called a preamplifier or serve some of the functions described above. Until the mid-1990s, there was much less confusion. Now, for example, one must choose between an Audio/Video Preamplifier (also known as a home theater controller, these include multi-channel and surround sound decoding and the ability to switch between multiple video as well as audio sources), a Line Level Preamplifier (which only accepts "line level" signals, such as from a CD player), or a more traditional preamp that includes both line level and a phono stage to play back LPs. Digital Preamps accept a digital signal, and incorporate a D/A converter to send the signal to an amplifier. Digital preamps often have an array of signal processing options not found—or even possible—on analog preamps. Most digital preamps will also accept analog signals, either functioning like an analog preamp and simply routing the signal, or sometimes converting the signal to digital and sending it through the digital circuitry, necessitating its conversion back to analog at some point down the chain. The analog signal of these latter preamps invariably degrades with this A/D-D/A conversion.

A Phono Preamp—which may be the phono stage of a fully functional preamp, or a separate component altogether—only accepts a signal from a phono cartridge, the voltage from which is significantly less than a line level signal. It then equalizes the signal to the RIAA curve, and boosts the level to approximately that of a line level source. A Pre-Preamplifier takes the signal presented by a moving coil (MC) cartridge, which is much less than moving magnet (MM) or moving iron cartridges, and boosts it to a level that can be used by a phono preamp.[5]

The most important consideration for a library when making a decision about amps and preamps is the construction quality. Do the moving parts—the volume control, switches, or buttons—have a solid feel, or do they seem like they will soon fall off? Do the input jacks into which interconnects from source components go fit their connections snugly, or are they loose? Do you feel that pushing too hard to insert the cables will break the back of the preamp?

Apart from these most outward signs of build quality, there are significant differences between brands and models in the quality of parts used inside the chassis. Perhaps the most crucial sonic part of a preamplifier is the quality of the volume control. A volume control determines how much of the available signal is fed to the amplification stage, and there are several designs in use today:

- Potentiometers (in audio jargon, "pots") sweep continuously from softest to loudest, and are usually found on the least expensive equipment. Not surprisingly, they are generally considered the most sonically inferior, although it should be noted that there are some well-made potentiometers. Pots are usually constructed of some kind of thin carbon film (although conductive plastic has also been occasionally used and found to be superior) or a wound coil, both of which have very poor audio characteristics. However, the better kinds of volume controls are almost never found on equipment within libraries' budgets.
- Stepped attenuators are often used in better equipment and are easily identified by their feel: a "notch" at each distinct volume level. There can be significant resistor noise in this design due to the noise of each resistor being added to each other, and the switch contacts degrade over time.[6]
- Ladder attenuators are similar to the stepped variety, but instead of numerous resistors in series, at any time only two resistors are active for a particular switch position. This design is more complicated and expensive to construct and is typically found only in high-end audio.

- Recently some high-end and studio audio manufacturers have been using a digital volume control designed and produced by Cirrus Logic, a leading chip manufacturer for DACs.[7] While this technology has not trickled down to mid-fi or inexpensive equipment, if it proves worthy over time then hopefully it will find its way into equipment libraries can afford.

Besides construction quality, there are other questions to resolve when looking for preamplifiers. Does the preamp have the flexibility that you need now and in the future? In particular, if you will be using a turntable with this preamp, does it have a proper input, and for the kind of cartridge: moving magnet/iron or moving coil? Are all of its functions available from the front panel, or do you need a remote control?

What functions does a library want in a preamp? There is a bewildering array of bells and whistles that some manufacturers include on their preamps. Perhaps the most useful button, one that seems to be disappearing from many preamps made today, is one that allows the user to make the stereo signal monophonic. This feature is helpful for recordings that were recorded monophonically, and either the LP is worn or the disc is a poorly engineered reissue—particularly, fake stereo reissues. In these instances, the mono button can greatly improve the listening experience.

Beyond a mono switch, a good rule of thumb is: the simpler a preamp the better.[8] Any kind of tone control beyond a treble and bass adjustment should be avoided. Indeed, even treble and bass knobs are a dubious necessity: they generally affect too broad a range to do more than distort the signal. A signal that passes through them, even in their neutral position, is not likely to emerge unscathed. On some equipment one can find a "bypass" or "direct" switch that keeps the signal from entering the tone controls. Some manufacturers have buttons or switches for circuits that are unique to them. For example, NAD has for many years included a "Soft Clipping" switch that helps when the unit is played at very loud levels. This is a proprietary circuit only found on NAD equipment.

The back of the preamp is at least as important as the front. Does it have enough inputs for the number of components that will be attached to it? What kind of input jacks does it have, not only the style of connector, but the metal out of which it is made? Most of the equipment that a library will employ will be connected by RCA connectors. Sonically, the problem with these connecting wires is that they are "unbalanced," and act as an antenna for all sorts of EM noise. A superior alternative is a balanced connection, which typically uses XLR connectors.[9] Professional audio components almost always use balanced connections to eliminate noise (especially ground noise) from the signal path. This becomes more important as the length of the cable increases; the short distance between components stacked in close proximity negates much of the advantage of balanced cables. Both the source component and the preamp must have balanced outputs/inputs, and many higher end audio components are starting to use balanced connections. Most consumer audio components do not use balanced connections, however, so in most instances this is not an option for libraries. Further, some audio components have been marketed that use XLR connectors, but are in fact unbalanced, single-ended designs. Although the noise-canceling properties of a balanced connection are not realized, XLRs are superior connectors to RCA plugs, and therefore at least some benefit is realized. A more thorough discussion of interconnects will be found in the last chapter.

Some preamps, primarily designed for the consumer home theater market, have different kinds of digital connectors, to take the digital output of a CD or DVD player and keep it in the digital domain until being converted to analog further along the chain. There are many advantages to this, depending on where the digital-to-analog conversion takes place, and the quality of those converters. Digital inputs and DACs are found on only a couple of preamplifiers aimed at the audio-only market, but it seems a likely future innovation. The most common digital connections are S/PDIF (Sony/Philips Digital Interface Format) and TosLink. S/PDIF connectors can be RCA plugs, coax (like cable TV), or even ⅛-inch mini-jacks; the cables carry the digital signal via a 75 Ω coaxial cable. TosLink, developed by Toshiba, uses an optical cable and one of two specific kinds of connector modules. This is discussed in further detail under interconnects.

While digital connections are starting to be found more often, preamps with a phono section are becoming scarcer. Indeed, it is almost impossible at this writing to find a preamp that both includes a phono section *and* costs less than $500.[10] However, a preamp without an integrated phono stage is not necessarily a bad thing. Since most consumers who are looking for preamplifiers that will allow them to use a turntable are also discriminating audiophiles, those few preamps that allow for this feature usually use at least an adequate phono stage. Only a few years ago many phono sections were almost throwaways for manufacturers, included only because it was expected rather than because they thought anyone would use them. If the preamp a library chooses does not include a phono input, one can purchase a separate unit—a phono preamp—that comes between a turntable and the preamp. The reason this is necessary is that the output of a turntable is significantly less than that of a CD player, tape deck, or other "line level" source. Fortunately, since no user controls need to be accessible once the unit is installed, this piece of equipment does not even need to be visible, if it is more convenient or aesthetically pleasing for it to be hidden. Today a few turntables (for example the Audio Technica AT-PL50) are even produced with their own preamplification built in.

As with any other piece of equipment, phono preamps range from very inexpensive (under $50), simplistic step-up devices to extremely expensive units costing several thousand dollars (the most expensive model today costs nearly $30,000). There are several phono preamps between $90 and $130 that are quite suitable for libraries. Some very inexpensive phono preamps, however, are only battery operated, without even an AC option.[11] The cheapest of phono preamps should be avoided as they typically are the noisiest, and often have inadequate power supplies, resulting in background hum. Just as we want preamps and amplifiers not to leave a sonic fingerprint, that is, to simply increase the voltage and current of the signal without distortion or noise, this should also be the goal of a phono preamp.

Care must be given, however, to match the phono preamp to the cartridge driving it, or vice versa. Cartridges vary significantly in the amount of voltage they put out. Moving magnet, moving iron, and high-output moving coil cartridges have a higher output—typically 2-8 mV, or millivolts—than do most moving coil cartridges, which range from under .5 mV to perhaps 2.5 mV. If the phono stage has too little gain for a particular cartridge, the overall volume of the preamp must be raised to make the signal loud enough, which increases the noise floor (the background hiss). If the cartridge output is too much, however, it can overload the phono circuitry, leading to distortion. The typical 1 kHz phono preamp gain for MM cartridges and the like is 37 to 40 dB.

Similarly, some attention should be paid to the compatibility between the preamp and both the source components and, where applicable, the amplifier. Generally, as discussed elsewhere in this book, specifications are not particularly helpful to us when looking for equipment. In the case of preamps, though, it is useful to pay attention to the amount of gain[12] a preamp yields. The typical gain from a preamp's line stage ranges from 5 to 25 dB, with 10-15 dB being optimal for most applications. If a preamp's gain is at the high end of that range, and a source component that has an exceptionally high output is connected to it, the result is that the volume control will be nearly nonfunctional, only the lowest levels being usable before the volume is too loud. Most volume controls do not perform their best at these settings, making it very difficult to make fine adjustments to the volume level.

Although typically only found in reviews, if at all, another specification worth looking for is RIAA equalization accuracy. If the preamp has a phono section, it is important to the sonic qualities of the records played through this circuit that the response be as flat as possible. Errors can be the result of poor design and/or poor tolerance matching of components. If the graph shows a dome-like curve, or significant roll off at either end of the spectrum, the capacitor tolerances in the RIAA circuit may be bad.[13] The best preamps maintain accurate RIAA ±0.1 dB, 20 Hz to 20 kHz, but even ±0.5 dB is not likely to be a problem in a library application.

Although headphone amps are really a kind of amplifier (discussed below), the fact that they just drive headphones make them a potential substitute for preamplifiers for library listening. Although a few come with multiple inputs, most headphone amps accept input from one line level source only, and have but a volume control and one or two headphone jacks on the front panel. There are several advantages to this approach. First, headphone amps are very minimal designs: most of the bells and whistles (including tone controls or balance) found on audio or home theater preamps will not appear on a headphone amp. All of the money spent on parts goes solely into raising the voltage and current of the input signal to the point where headphones can be played. If a high quality volume control is used, the results can be very transparent. Second, without a lot of circuitry needed inside, headphone amps are usually smaller than a typical preamp. A good headphone amp will not necessarily be any cheaper than a fully functional preamplifier, but most of the cost is in quality parts and construction.

There are many plans available for constructing headphone amps, and it might be worth looking into having custom headphone amps made. One of the most obvious advantages to this would be the possibility of constructing them with a ⅛-inch mini-jack instead of the standard ¼-inch. Very few headphones made today terminates in a ¼-inch plug, and therefore mini-to-¼-inch adapters are used. In most libraries, the rate of loss of these adapters is not insignificant, and libraries would welcome eliminating the need for adapters.

It is worth noting here that the full effect of a high quality DVD cannot be gained without some way to be enveloped in surround sound. Home installations use an A/V receiver and multiple speakers, which may not be practical in a library. In a home theater application, the A/V receiver is the "brains" of the system, taking various inputs from both audio and video components, and routing their signals to the intended outputs (speakers or a monitor). Unless a library is providing a surround sound listening environment, an A/V receiver is unnecessary. Presently, there are very few surround headphones made, and those that have come to market are aimed at video gamers, not at audiophiles or for music.[14]

If surround sound is in a library's plans, then it is important to understand the different varieties of surround sound, as discussed in the previous chapter. DVDs may employ one and sometime multiple surround sound formats, and the receiver must be able to decode the signal and route the correct channel to the appropriate speaker. There are five basic surround sound schemes used today, most of them invented by Dolby Labs. Dolby Surround is the consumer version of Dolby Stereo, which is heard in many theaters. A stereo signal is separated into three channels: front left and right, and rear center (multiple rear speakers will play the same signal). This is the most basic and one of the oldest surround schemes. Dolby Pro-Logic enhanced Dolby Surround by adding a front center channel for better audibility of speech. The rear speakers are still fed a monophonic signal.

In 1991, Dolby released Dolby Digital which added a subwoofer signal for Low Frequency Effects (LFE), and made the two rear channels into a stereo pair. This is what is commonly known today as "5.1 surround" and sometimes referred to as "AC-3." Another important distinction is that Dolby Digital is truly a digital soundtrack, whereas Dolby Surround and Pro-Logic are encoded as analog. Dolby Digital is the surround format chosen as the standard for HDTV. Next on the multi-channel horizon is "7.1," which adds two more discrete audio channels. This format has already made an impact in the computer gaming market.[15] Dolby Digital EX is very similar to Dolby Digital, with the addition of a separate rear center channel, but is relatively little used at this time.

The one notable non-Dolby surround format is DTS (Digital Theater Sound). DTS (the name of the company and the system) is a proprietary surround system backed initially by Universal. By the mid-1990s, DTS had developed consumer electronics applications, and has been widely accepted by many movie studios for their video releases. DTS is now also widely used on DVD-Audio discs. There are now several "flavors" of DTS. The original is 5.1, much like AC-3. When Dolby/THX[16] released their 6.1 format (THX Surround EX, which added a center rear channel), DTS responded with DTS-ES, which itself has two versions: discrete and matrix. DTS-ES matrix requires a special chip to decode a rear channel signal that is encoded with the left and right rear signals, whereas the discrete version gives each channel its own track. There is much more involved in setting up a proper surround sound or home theater listening environment than purchasing the necessary equipment, but that topic is beyond the scope of this book.[17]

## Amplifiers

Unless speakers are the sound producers of an audio system, libraries are better served purchasing either a headphone amp or preamplifier to power headphones. All other things being equal, it is wasted money to purchase a product that will not be used in the way it was intended. Between a $300 preamplifier and an integrated amplifier at the same price, the preamp should have better construction quality and parts. However, some reasonably priced integrated amplifiers offer the phono preamp that preamplifiers in that same price range do not.

Audiophiles consider amplifiers as discreet pieces of equipment. For the purposes of this discussion, however, the issues of amplification are the same whether considering an integrated amplifier or an amplifier as a separate unit, used with a preamplifier.[18] The amplifier is typically the piece of equipment most devoid of "features," at least those over which a user has some control.[19] As such, the difference between amps lies mostly in their parts quality and engineering design.

The basic concept of an amplifier, as its name suggests, is to boost the input signal to the point where the signal can be converted by speakers from electrical to acoustic energy. To accomplish that, however, requires several different steps (or stages), involving a number of different components inside. Engineer John Linsley Hood writes, "The ultimate requirement of an amplifier is that it should feed power to loudspeakers. This is the most difficult of the purely electronic portions of the sound reproduction system."[20] The important thing about an amplifier, though, is that it requires energy beyond the original signal in order to boost it enough. Typically, although this is a gross oversimplification, an audio amplifier will take power from the incoming AC, convert it to DC to make the current even, and use this to increase the voltage and current of the output signal. The lower the impedance of the speakers, the more current is necessary. A byproduct of this process is heat; the more power used and generated, the more heat is produced. Because they dissipate the heat generated by their considerable power supplies with large heatsinks, most audiophile amplifiers tend to be very large and heavy (expensive should go without saying). Unless powering speakers to fill a very large room or auditorium, libraries will not require amplifiers of that magnitude. Nevertheless, all amplifiers need some space surrounding them.

There are many measurements provided in an effort to compare amplifiers. Power output,[21] input impedance, THD, sensitivity, and so on are usually emblazoned on product literature. They are also relatively meaningless as far as a determining purchasing factor. Taken by themselves and looking at one particular amplifier, a little bit of knowledge might be gained if you know how to interpret these numbers, but there are four principle problems:

- The manufacturer rarely indicates what kind of testing produced the figures, nor would most consumers understand even if they did.
- Such measurements may not reflect how the amp will react to real music, which presents anything but a continuous voltage.
- Correlations between a given electrical measurement and an amplifier's subjective sound quality have never been established.[22]
- Any *one* measurement does not indicate that a given unit is better than another: a 50 W amplifier from one company may sound much better than a 250 W amp from another.

Further, some measurements, such as THD, were more useful many years ago when engineers were still learning how to bias and properly use feedback to push distortion to inaudible levels.[23] Using THD as an example, though, some manufacturers in the 1970s and '80s began to do whatever they could to reduce THD to astonishingly low levels—which looked good to those in marketing and on brochures—but they accomplished this technical feat at the expense of sound quality.

One thing that differentiates power amplifiers from other parts of the audio chain is the fact that it is possible for an amp to be incompatible with the speakers it is driving. The one measurement to which one should pay attention is the impedance (a measurement of a circuit's total opposition to the flow of AC, measured in ohms). Amplifiers and speakers have impedances generally ranging from 4 to 8 $\Omega$. The lower the figure, the more current is drawn from the amplifier. While an amp that comfortably drives 8 $\Omega$ speakers usually can drive a 4 $\Omega$ speaker at low or moderate levels, increasing the volume raises the risk of damaging both amp and speaker. The amplifier must have enough output current to drive the lowest impedance presented to it by the speaker. However, loudspeakers do not have flat impedance curves, because impedance varies with frequency in reactive loads, which is what a speaker presents to the amplifier. Reactances are actually more difficult to drive than pure resistances, which is typically what is presented to an amplifier when tested and therefore why bench tests can be deceiving.

Another marketing term found in amplifier literature is "high current." In the abstract, an amplifier with more current is better than one with less. More current requires a larger power supply, but allows such an amplifier to provide more power to the speaker with the same voltage (or input).[24] The higher the output current, the lower the output impedance, giving such amplifiers the ability to drive low-impedance reactive loads. However, "high current" is not an absolute or a standard, and thus two amps may measure the same but only one labeled by its manufacturer as high current.

How much power do you need? That has always been a significant question when looking at amplifiers. As Robert Harley notes:

> Choosing an appropriate amplifier power-output for your loudspeakers, listening tastes, room, and budget is essential to getting the best sound for your money. If the amplifier is under-powered for your needs, you'll never hear the system at its full potential. The sound will be constricted, fatiguing, lack dynamics, and the music will have a sense of strain on climaxes.[25]

Harley also points out that many factors determine power needs, including the sensitivity of the loudspeaker used (the most critical dynamic), impedance (mentioned above), and the room in which the equipment will play. Speaker sensitivity is a measurement of how much sound (measured in decibels) a speaker produces for a given power input (measured in watts) at a given distance, (usually 1 m). Each 3 dB increase in SPL (Sound Pressure Level) requires a doubling of the power. For a speaker measuring 88 dB SPL at 1 W/1 m to get to 91 dB SPL, the power must be doubled to 2 W. To attain a reasonable level of 109 dB SPL, the amplifier must output 128 W of power. By the same token, a speaker that starts out at 91 dB will only require 64 W of power from an amp to reach that same 109 dB SPL. While it may seem that the second speaker is "only" slightly more sensitive, a much less powerful amplifier is required to drive it to realistic listening levels.[26] The effect, then, is that the requirements of the speaker determine what amplifier to purchase.

Comparing the power ratings of amplifiers is not straightforward. As mentioned above, manufacturers often apply different criteria or characteristics to their test measurements, and what may appear to be comparative specifications may in fact be quite different. Indeed, manufacturers' attempts to exaggerate the power their amplifiers delivered became so misleading that in 1974 the Federal Trade Commission (FTC) passed a regulation concerning the advertising of power ratings (16 CFR Part 432, *Rule Relating to Power Output Claims for Amplifiers Utilized in Home Entertainment Products*[27]). That is now one of two kinds of ratings commonly found, the other being from the Electronic Industries Association (EIA). The FTC rating is the more useful of the two, specifying that the power rating be measured continuously driving both channels over a specified frequency range at no more than the stated THD. The power rating is sometimes referred to as RMS, or "root mean square", and is differentiated from "peak"-only measurement. The specified frequency range should be 20 Hz to 20 kHz, but when it benefits the manufacturer is sometimes advertised at a higher low frequency such as 50 Hz. The EIA standard only calls for rating a single channel driven at one frequency, usually 1 kHz. This kind of power rating can be up to 30% higher than an FTC rating for the same unit, so it is important to be sure when comparing specifications that the measurements were done the same.

To return to the question of how much power or wattage one needs, the answer is: it all depends. What size room will the amplifier attempt to fill? A small listening room will have very modest requirements. How efficient are the speakers? Most libraries will not be using exotic speakers, and therefore the demands that the speakers place on the amplifier may not be great. Further, unless the room is completely acoustically isolated, more power simply invites listeners to turn the volume up to levels that may disturb others in the vicinity. With these caveats in mind, anything between 20 and 60 W *should* be adequate.

One of the most confusing aspects of amplifiers has to do with their class. It is easy to assume, especially for non-engineers, that if an amp is "Class A" it must be better than "Class B" and that "Class A-B" should be somewhere in between. However, in the case of amplifiers, "class" refers to the state of their output transistors. Amplifiers are typically push-pull designs, where one transistor (or a parallel set of transistors) amplifies the positive-going half of the audio waveform, and the other transistor (or parallel set) amplifies the negative-going portion. Push-pull amplification reduces distortion.

In a Class B design, the signal is passed from one transistor to the next, each turning off when no signal is presented. Sonically, there are two problems with this design. First, there is a distortion or "notch" at the point where one transistor stops and the other begins. Second, most transistors are not linear immediately when they begin, which leads to distortions, and only become linear during the time they are on. Class A-B amps, the most common variety found, try to solve these problems by overlapping slightly the time when the transistors are operating. Class A amps feature transistors that are always conducting. This design is favored by many high-end designers because distortion is virtually immeasurable, but Class A amplifiers are usually large, hot to the touch, and complex to design well.[28] Class A-B amps are much more efficient, and typically can be made more powerful. Further, they operate in Class A at low levels to take advantage of the sonic qualities that Class A transistor modes allow, and switch to B for higher level signals. This keeps the amp cooler and allows for smaller designs.

In recent years, many of the better-designed solid-state amplifiers have used Field Effect Transistors (FETs), and more specifically MOS-FETs, or Metal Oxide Semiconductor Field Effect Transistors, instead of bipolar transistors for the output stage. MOSFETs have some significant advantages over standard transistors, including better resistance to high temperatures and radiation (making them much more durable), the ability to accept a tremendous amount of current, faster switching (which reduces crossover distortion), and simply less noise.[29] When reading specifications of amplifiers or preamplifiers, the inclusion of MOSFETs *usually*—certainly not always—indicates a better piece of equipment.

The other parts of an amplifier that will distinguish better equipment are the binding posts, where the speaker wire is connected on the back of the unit. There are two common varieties of terminals, both on amplifiers and speakers: spring-loaded and five-way binding posts. The former are usually found on cheaper equipment, the latter on better. Five-way binding posts are superior in their ability to provide a solid connection between the wire and terminal, have more surface-to-surface contact, and accept a wider variety of speaker wire terminations (which will be discussed below).[30] Not only the kind of binding posts, but the metal out of which they are made can determine quality. Gold-plated binding posts not only conduct the signal better, but also resist oxidation, which, over the years, ultimately degrades the ability of the signal to move from the amplifier to the speaker wire.

One of the interesting—or not, if you are not so inclined—audiophile arguments one comes across is whether or not amplifiers should ever be turned off. The theory posited by those who advocate leaving electronics on is that the equipment is "warmed up" and ready for intense listening at all times. Many audiophiles believe that equipment needs to be warmed up to sound its best. There are many others who believe just as strongly that turning equipment off and on makes no difference at all to the sound quality. It is worth noting, however, that the FTC power ratings require that the amplifier have a "warm up" period before testing commences. There is a strong correlation between how high end the equipment is of the person who advocates leaving components on, and how strongly they argue the point. Assuming it is even possible to keep users from turning equipment off, there are more potential negatives than positives to leaving equipment on.

Finally, mention should be made of "digital amplifiers." In most instances, reference to an amplifier being digital is somewhat misleading. An amp may, in fact, accept a digital signal from a preamp or other source component, but then the signal is just processed through the amp's DACs, at which point the signal is handled by a traditional amplifier. The only advantage gained with this model is that the digital-to-analog conversion does not take place until immediately before amplification. Assuming the digital signal is still intact, it successfully avoids spending a longer period of time in the analog domain which is generally a good thing.

However, a number of engineers are working on truly digital amplifiers in which the signal is never converted to analog. PCM data is converted to PWM data, which, after some manipulations, is used to drive directly the output transistors of an amplifier. The potential audio advantages are enormous, but to date few such amplifiers have been brought to market, and those have been very expensive (the TacT Audio Millennium MKII is over $10,000). This might very well prove to be the next technological breakthrough in audio design.

## Notes

1. A possible third part of the chain is sometimes referred to as the "pre-preamplifier" (also called a "head amplifier"), a step-up transformer that is used to boost the gain of a phono cartridge to a level that a typical preamplifier can use (see the previous discussion of cartridges).

2. John J. Adams, "How an Amplifier Works," *Complete Guide to Audio* (Indianapolis: Howard W. Sams, 1998), 52.

3. Further confounding matters for audiophiles, but not typically for libraries, is the decision about whether to use vacuum tube technology (often preferred for its "warmth" or "musicality" of sound) or solid state electronics. Libraries universally choose the latter, and rightfully so.

4. Mention should also be made of the "passive" preamp, or more correctly, the "passive level control." For line level equipment that has enough gain to drive interconnects plus an amplifier, and therefore does not need its voltage increased, a "passive" preamp can simply pass the signal through without doing anything active. A switch is included to change between source components, and an overall volume control, but active circuitry is not used. Unfortunately, there are apparently no commercially available passive preamps that include a headphone jack. Further, most provide very limited switching capabilities (one or two components at the most). Sonically, however, a passive level control should be superior to an active preamp simply because there are fewer circuits, transistors, capacitors, and so forth through which the audio signal must travel.

5. A step-up transformer performs the same function, but uses a transformer instead of an active circuit.

6. For a very technical discussion of stepped attenuators, see "How Stepped Attenuators Work," n.d., <http://www.goldpt.com/how.html> (October 27, 2004).

7. For more information and a circuit diagram of the Crystal CS3310, please see "Stereo Digital Volume Control," July 2004, <http://www.cirrus.com/en/pubs/proDatasheet/CS3310.pdf> (October 20, 2004).

8. Gary Galo, audio engineer at the Crane School of Music, SUNY at Potsdam, and co-chair of the Association for Recorded Sound Collections Technical Committee from 1996 to 2004, has designed and built custom pre-amplifiers for the Crane Music Library. One of his primary goals was to make the preamp as simple and "foolproof" as possible. His detailed article about it appeared in *audioXpress* ("A Music Library Preamp," *audioXpress Magazine*, March 2005, 24-35).

9. Balanced connections can also be terminated in a ¼ in TRS plug, but these are found almost solely on professional equipment.

10. I am aware of only one such preamp, made by Parasound and retailing for about $250. The NAD C-162 is the next closest in price at nearly $600.

11. The Radio Shack Magnetic Cartridge Stereo Preamp, catalog number 970-1018 ($25), for example, requires just a 9 V battery. However, most battery-operated phono preamps do not have as much gain or headroom as AC-powered units, and of course they require periodic battery replacement.

12. Gain is the amount the signal is increased from the time it enters the preamp to the time it is sent to the IC op-amp or discreet transistor amplifier.

13. Harley, 149.

14. There is one headphone made that might prove worth investigating for those libraries that do not offer surround sound loudspeaker listening: the Zalman Theatre6 5.1 Surround Sound Headphone, model ZM-RS6F. Initially aimed at gamers with multi-channel sound cards in their PCs, Zalman is now trying to breach the audio/video market. They have introduced a headphone amplifier, model ZM-RSA, required to connect the headphone with an A/V receiver (the headphone has three connectors). I have not listened to them, and thus cannot comment on their sound or build quality. For more information see <http://www.zalmanusa.com>.

15. At the time of this writing, very little content is available that uses all eight channels. Therefore software is used to blend 5.1 encoded (or even stereo) audio into 7.1 output, creating a faux soundfield.

16. THX is not a surround format, but rather a standard that must be met in order to be certified as THX.

17. A professional surround sound installer should be hired to do this work.

18. For a very readable explanation of amplifier design and components, see Rod Elliott, *Amplifier Basics: How Audio Amps Work*, June 9, 2001, <http://sound.westhost.com/amp-basics.htm> (July 10, 2003).

19. Perhaps the one notable exception is the "Soft Clipping" switch found on most NAD amps and integrated amplifiers. Even this feature, though, is not something that is switched on and off regularly. Since NAD products are often found in libraries because of their excellent price-to-performance ratio, it is worth noting here. "Clipping" refers to the effect when an amp is over-driven, past the point to which it was designed. If one were to look at a rounded sine wave picture, clipping looks like the peaks have been chopped off, or flattened

out. All amplifiers "clip" at some point (and typically the less powerful the amp, the earlier the onset of clipping as one turns up the volume), and it is more audible with some than with others. NAD's circuit makes the clipping "less hard" (hence the name) and easier on the ears. Clipping was much more of an audible artifact of transistorized amplifiers, even into the late 1980s, but current circuit design and the use of FETs have masked or reduced the effect on better-quality components.

20. John Linsley Hood, "Power Output Stages," in *Audio and Hi-Fi Handbook*, edited by Ian R.Sinclair, rev. 3rd ed (Oxford: Newnes, 2000), 252.

21. Power is measured in watts, often shown as watts/channel or W/ch, usually into a certain number of ohms, e.g. 125 watts continuous @ (or into) 4 Ω (20 Hz and 20 kHz). Often promotional literature will tout a figure for total wattage, which must then be divided by the number of channels. The FTC requires that power output per channel be listed in the official specifications for a unit. Although speaker manufacturers will often specify minimum requirements for amplifier wattage, this is significant only for inefficient speakers such as acoustic suspension.

22. For a good list of measurable performance characteristics of amplifiers and the difficulties of connecting those measurements to perceived sound, see Rod Elliot, *Amplifier Sound: What Are the Influences*, February 27, 2000, <http://sound.westhost.com/amp-sound.htm> (July 11, 2003). This is one of the main reasons why reviews that rely solely on measurements, such as those typically found in *Stereo Review*, are particularly meaningless for assessing the sound quality of a given piece of equipment.

23. One measurement that could be important is an amplifier's "gain" in comparison to another's, but this is only important if the two amplifiers will be used to "bi-amplify" a pair of speakers. However, many audiophiles do not bi-amplify their speakers, and it seems unlikely that any library will go to that trouble.

24. Mathematically, the power of an amplifier (measured in watts) is derived from multiplying the voltage by the current ($P=E2/Z$). By increasing the current, the amplifier is made more powerful, at least on paper.

25. Harley, 157.

26. Ibid., 157-58.

27. Federal Trade Commission, 16 CFR Part 432, *Trade Regulation Rule Relating to Power Output Claims for Amplifiers Utilized in Home Entertainment Products*, 2000, <http://www.ftc.gov/os/2000/12/amplifierrulefrn.pdf> (October 31, 2003).

28. Theoretically there are also two other classes of amplifiers: C and D. Class C amps are only used for radio frequencies (although at least one audio amp employed Class C circuitry for part of its design). Class D amplifiers had a brief flourish in the late 1970s, marketed as "digital" amplifiers by Sony and a few other manufacturers. Their poor sound qualities soon pushed them out of the marketplace for most audio applications.

29. Much of the background noise from bipolar transistors comes from the fact that electrons must flow through a PN junction, whereas FETs, as unipolar transistors, allow current to flow through only a P- or N-channel. For a more

technical explanation, see Alan A. Cohen, "Semiconductors," *Audio Technology Fundamentals* (Indianapolis, IN: Howard W. Sams, 1989), 129-50.

30. For more about the two different terminals, see "Speaker Bindings: Connecting to the Amplifier," n.d., <http://www.audiovideo101.com/learn/articles/speakers/speakers18.asp> (October 28, 2004).

# CHAPTER 5

# SOUND PRODUCERS

## Loudspeakers

Loudspeakers are the end of the audio chain. An electrical signal, hopefully not too different from that which the medium played at the beginning of the audio chain, is taken in from the speaker wire and sent by the crossover network to one or more drivers that convert that signal from electrical energy to acoustic energy.[1] As the piece of equipment that actually produces the sound one hears, many have felt that loudspeakers are the most important component in the audio chain. As I hope has been made clear in previous chapters, there are no unimportant parts to the chain, and any weak link can negate the superb audio characteristics of the equipment before or after.

"Drivers" are the actual transducers, the components that generate the physical sound waves. Most speaker drivers are electrodynamic, more fully spelled out as "moving coil electrodynamic loudspeaker" but usually just referred to as "dynamic." They employ a permanent magnet to pump a cone back and forth. The pumping of the cone moves the surrounding air at different frequencies and amplitudes, re-creating—to a greater or lesser degree—the sounds that were picked up originally by the microphone. Within the general rubric of dynamic speakers there are several flavors, including vented (or bass reflex), acoustic suspension, transmission line, aperiodic, and passive radiator.

The other form of speaker is the "flat panel," which comes in many varieties, including the electrostatic and planar magnetic.[2] Some speakers combine elements of a panel design: a ribbon or electrostatic driver for the mid- and high-range frequencies and a dynamic cone driver for the bass frequency. Although both the planar and hybrid designs are popular among audiophiles for their clarity and superior transient response, these kinds of speakers have some significant disadvantages as far as library usage is concerned:

- They typically have very low impedances, making amplifier matching more difficult.

- They are not as sensitive, therefore requiring more powerful amplifiers to play at the same dynamic levels as conventional speakers.
- They are usually larger than dynamic speakers, and more difficult to place within a room—usually well away from the back wall—for best results, making them less flexible.
- They can be more susceptible to damage.
- Electrostatic speakers require AC power.
- Panel speakers tend to be expensive.

Given these limitations, only dynamic speakers seem appropriate for library use, and the rest of the discussion will refer just to them.[3]

Conventional loudspeakers have four elements: the connectors and internal wiring, the passive crossover network, the drivers (which may number from two to several), and the cabinet that holds everything. Beginning with the latter, there are two primary kinds of cabinets.[4] Both types seek to solve an engineering problem by very different means. The problem is that after a cone pushes out, causing sound to emanate into the room, it also must fall back into place, causing a duplicate sound wave to move backwards towards the rear of the speaker. These two radiations are of opposite polarity, described as being 180° "out-of-phase." If these waves mix, they cancel each other, which is why there must be some kind of enclosure. The methods of addressing this issue are called "loading." One type of cabinet tries to eliminate or absorb all of the rear radiation, and the other tries to make use of that same acoustic energy.

The acoustic suspension kind of cabinet, also sometimes referred to as "air suspension" or "closed box," with the "infinite baffle"[5] and "Isobarik"[6] designs being somewhat related, is entirely sealed, keeping the sound waves inside the speaker. There are certain problems encountered by trapping all of that acoustic energy in such a small space (especially lower frequencies, which have larger sound waves). Speakers whose sound only radiates to the front are sometimes called "point source" speakers, but that term should really be used only to describe speakers that attempt to force all of the sound radiation from one point, a difficult task with multiple drivers.

The other kind of enclosure is called vented, "ported box" or, more rarely, "phase inverter." Instead of completely sealing the rear wave inside, a vented speaker has a port, or a small opening, that releases that acoustic energy into the room. By tuning this port properly, the rear wave is released in phase with the front wave. Vented speakers are a descendant of the bass reflex design, but take advantage of the mathematical calculations of Thiele and Small for more predictable results.[7]

A "passive radiator" design is similar to the vented enclosure in that a second, passive driver is coupled to the active woofer and thus serves the same acoustic function as a port.

As with all such competing designs, there are vocal adherents to both kinds. Many feel that, all things being equal, a sealed system does not go as low as a vented system before it starts to "roll off" (something that all drivers do as they go lower in their range). The point at which the roll off begins is called the "low frequency cutoff point." However, once the vented system begins to roll off, its descent is twice as steep. The impression one has listening to two such designs is that the sealed design is usually described as "fuller," the vented design as "louder." Bass reflex designs also tend to be more sensitive, requiring less amplifier power to drive, which is why they were so popular in the 1950s and 1960s when amplifiers were not as powerful as they became.

Besides the method of loading, the other significant difference between dynamic speaker cabinets is the material out of which they are constructed as well as how well braced they are inside. The ideal cabinet would be completely inert, and the ways that speaker manufacturers have tried to produce such a cabinet are as varied as the human imagination. Realistically, though, every material will resonate to a greater or lesser degree, and each has its own "natural resonant frequency." Cabinet vibrations, though narrow in frequency and without as much acoustic energy as the sound produced by a driver, alter the music's tonal color. Further, the larger the cabinet, the more difficult it is to dampen unwanted vibrations. When judging speakers, as with turntables, knock on various parts of the cabinet and listen for a dull sound; a hollow or ringing sound indicates a poorly dampened speaker that should be avoided. Most speaker cabinets are constructed with Medium Density Fiberboard (MDF) to which a wood veneer is laminated.

There are up to three kinds of drivers found in conventional, full-range speakers: tweeter, mid-range, and woofer. Sometimes the mid-range is not found, but the tweeter and woofer will be present. The tweeter handles the high frequencies and is the smallest; the mid-range obviously radiates the middle frequencies; and the woofer (the largest cone) the lowest, or bass notes. One also finds speakers where multiple tweeters and mid-range drivers and occasionally woofers exist in the same cabinet.

Usually found as a separate speaker is the "subwoofer," which only handles the very lowest frequencies (approximately 20 to 150 Hz). A subwoofer, or "sub," is a mainstay in home theater systems to accentuate special effects.[8] Sounds in this region of the audio spectrum are omni-directional, and therefore the subwoofer's placement in the room is not critical to the spatial relation of the rest of the sounds. The sub-woofer is a separate speaker for several reasons:

- The amount of air that such low frequencies must move is so great that incorporating it into a regular speaker enclosure would make that cabinet enormous.
- Only one subwoofer is generally required to get the full effect.
- Better-designed subwoofers are "active" (rather than "passive") and have their own integrated power amp and crossover.
- Subwoofers isolate low frequency vibrations from the driver and enclosure that reproduces the mid-range. Adding a subwoofer can improve the mid-range and treble as much as the bass.

Generally speaking, it is difficult to imagine a library situation where a subwoofer is appropriate. Unless the library is setting up home theater viewing rooms, there is no reason to consider a subwoofer. The very low frequencies that are produced by the subwoofer are those that are most difficult to contain in a room, and most likely to travel throughout a building as vibrations. Indeed, musically there is almost nothing to be gained by a subwoofer, but much to be lost. Subwoofers can be difficult to integrate properly with two full-range speakers.

The third component of a speaker is a series of filters that form the crossover, or dividing, network. Since speaker drivers are not full frequency (20 Hz – 20 kHz), the crossover network needs to take the incoming signal and send the right frequencies to the right drivers. There are overlaps between drivers, of course, so that the crossover region from driver to driver should appear seamless. The engineering skill that goes into the crossover network is perhaps the largest determinant of a speaker's success or failure.

Crossovers are referred to by their "order": first, second, third, and fourth order. Each describes the mathematical relationship of the "cutoff frequency" (the frequency at which signals are sent to one driver or another) to the "slope" (how gradual or steep the roll off is beyond that cutoff point).[9] As one progresses from first order to fourth order, the slope increases. A first-order crossover, then, has a greater overlap of frequencies between drivers, for example between a tweeter and mid-range. Since each driver is adept only at a certain range of frequencies, it is possible that frequencies either too low or too high for that driver to produce will be sent to it. However, the steeper the slope the more difficult it becomes to keep the "timing" correct between drivers, especially between the highest and lowest frequencies (that is, one driver may produce its sound fractionally before or after another driver). This is crudely equivalent to an ensemble where the trombones produce their notes a little slower than the flutes, which in turn are faster than the saxophones: the result of this mistiming is a muddied sound. In this way, crossovers are much like the conductor trying to get each member to play at precisely the right instant. The mathematical computations that go into determining optimal crossover patterns for specific design criteria are formidable.

What, if any, measurable specifications are worth considering when comparing speakers? While speaker measurements tend to be more telling than measurements of other components, some are more important than others.[10] As mentioned in the amplifier discussion, speakers come in a variety of impedances. This measurement is important because it determines how difficult the speakers are to drive, from the amplifier's point of view. The lower the measured impedance, the harder the amplifier must work. Similarly, a speaker with low sensitivity (mentioned in the amplifier discussion above) will also require more of the amplifier than a more sensitive speaker. A third measurable characteristic, phase angle, is not always included in a speaker's spec sheet because it usually is not expressed as a simple number. However, as a measurement of a speaker's reactance, it is another indicator of how easy or difficult a speaker is to drive. The flatter the phase angle, or the lower the number of degrees (e.g. $\pm 20°$), the easier an amplifier will be able to handle a particular loudspeaker.

Speaker reviews are often full of spectral decay graphs and frequency response curves. These can indeed be useful, as they can show where a speaker might be excessively resonant, where certain response non-linearities appear, or if there is severe roll off at the top or bottom of the range. However, one must take the time to understand what they mean and how to interpret them.[11] Ultimately, though, there is no substitute for listening. As John Watkinson writes, "The only criterion we have for the accuracy of a loudspeaker is the sensitivity of the human hearing system.... Consequently it beho[o]ves loudspeaker designers to study psychoacoustics in order to establish suitable performance criteria."[12] How a particular speaker matches with a given amplifier can only be discerned by putting them together and sending a signal through them.

A final consideration when comparing loudspeakers is that simpler is often better, especially with less expensive equipment. A more complex speaker—that is, one with more drivers, a more elaborate crossover, etc.—requires much more engineering and production skill. Given two speakers at the same price by two reputable manufacturers, the one with a simpler design often will have better cabinetry and/or higher quality components. Which one sounds better is in the ears of the listener.

Audiophiles will spend hours manipulating the placement of their speakers in a room, and for good reason. If speakers are carefully set up within a room, the listening experience is greatly enhanced: the stereo image snaps into place, location of musicians can be discerned, and the full effect of the recording is revealed. Conversely, without attention to this detail, the sound coming from the speakers is just so much noise. In particular, the higher the frequencies, the more directional they are. This is why subwoofers can be placed almost anywhere. Unfortunately, libraries rarely have the luxury of placing speakers optimally in a room.[13] If the library cannot ensure that their speakers will be set up properly, then it makes more fiscal sense to look at details of the equipment, such as warranties or construction quality, rather than how they sound.[14]

An important detail about speaker setup is to make sure that the polarity of each speaker is correctly matched with the amplifier. Speaker wire is discussed in more detail below, but for discussion here it is relevant to note that speaker wire is really two wires, generally coated red and black. It is imperative that the red wire be connected to the positive sides of both the amplifier and speaker, which are usually also red, sometimes marked with a "+," and that the black wire be connected to the negative, usually black, or "−." If one of these connections is reversed, sounds from one speaker will cancel the other out. This is often described as speakers being "out of phase" but is perhaps more accurately referred to as being of "opposite polarity."

Loudspeakers have traditionally been an analog device. A not unexpected result of the marketing of the word "digital" is that we now see "Digital Speaker Systems" (DSS). These speakers can accept a digital signal, either from a receiver/amplifier or directly from a source component such as a DVD player, and the signal is processed internally before being converted to an analog signal and sent to the drivers. One advantage to such speakers is that the DSP (Digital Signal Processing) can be customized to the performance characteristics of the particular speaker, and indeed replace the crossover network. Regardless of claims, however, inside the speaker's cabinet there must still be at least one DAC and amplifier in order to send the analog electrical signal to the drivers.[15] The more complex digital speakers utilize a DAC and amplifier for each driver (which means that the designer can customize each amp to a specific and known driver). While these speakers have yet to make much of a dent in the marketplace (except with personal computer speakers), they are the next logical link to replace in the analog chain.

# Headphones

Putting something onto or into one's ear to listen to sound is nothing new, dating back to early telephone and telegraph transmissions (not to mention ear trumpets, which have been used by the hard-of-hearing for centuries). However, it was not until the late 1950s and the introduction of stereo that the headphone began to be marketed as a separate piece of audio equipment. The emergence of Sony's Walkman not only spurred headphone development but spawned generations whose primary listening was done through headphones, not speakers.

Although the function of headphones and speakers is the same—both convert an electrical signal to acoustic energy in the form of sound waves—the way our brain perceives them is quite different due to the proximity of headphones to our ears. Loudspeakers must contend with the acoustics of the room, and in better situations are enhanced by them, whereas the sound generated by headphones of course has almost no acoustic interaction.

Headphone designers face the difficulty that most material listened to through headphones was originally meant and engineered for loudspeaker reproduction. Successful headphone design then must not only account for this discrepancy, but must also deal with "other aspects of human hearing, such as the occlusion effect, ambient noise attenuation, bone conduction, interaural attenuation and leak susceptibility."[16] Because the sheer volume of air between the transducer and ear canal is so small, compared to the volume of a room in which loudspeakers are played, and since the size of headphone transducers are comparatively small, true bass cannot be heard—much less felt—through this kind of listening experience.[17] Therefore, those listeners for whom headphones are their primary means of sound reproduction never experience true high fidelity, nor are they given the full experience of the music. Moreover, because there is little or no acoustic interaction with the surrounding environment, the subjective quality of the audio will be different for every user based on the fit of the phones and shape of the ear canal.

There are basically four kinds of headphones, all defined by the kind of seal against the listener's ear:

- **Circumaural** (closed seal) headphones try to completely eliminate any outside sounds.
- **Supra-aural** (semi-open or semi-closed, sometimes referred to in the British press as "velocity") allow some external sounds to penetrate to the listener.

- **Open-style** headphones (such as those typically found with portable equipment, sometimes called mini-earphones) make no attempt at reducing external sounds.
- **Intra-aural** (inner-ear, also including "ear bud") headphones do not rest on the outside of the ear, but are inserted directly into the ear canal.

Of these designs, circumaural headphones best reproduce the bass region, since they have the least amount of leakage, and for the same reason are better at keeping out unwanted sound. Moreover, from the designer's standpoint, closed headphones are more dependable because their positioning over the ears will be more consistent, compared to more open styles, between listeners. Closed headphones are the overwhelming choice for professionals, but they tend to be heavier and press more on the listener's head. In a library, listeners may not be able to listen as long as with other types. Design of the ear cushion is important, not only for comfort but for audible reasons. Some designs even use fluid-filled cushions for the ultimate in sealing. Image location—the ability to visualize each instrument in its proper space—is psychoacoustically different between closed and open designs.[18]

Supra-aural headphones are much lighter in weight, and usually preferred by listeners. However, like open-style headphones, not only do outside sounds enter through the porous earcushions, but, when played at high volume levels, the sound from these phones will also leak into the surrounding area. This can, of course, disturb other readers in a library setting. It should be noted here that over time, listening to headphones at loud volume levels will permanently damage a listener's ears. Studies have shown that people tend to listen to headphones louder than they listen to loudspeakers.[19] While there seems little a library can realistically do to guard listeners against this, it is a health issue about which listeners should be more aware.

Open headphones are typically found with portable equipment. Light enough to wear for several hours at a stretch, one of their disadvantages in libraries is that they also leak the most sound, both to the listener from external sources and to the surrounding area when played even at moderate levels. This may not be such a problem when used in a listening room that's acoustically isolated from the rest of the library. There are a few styles of open headphones to consider. The traditional style has one or two metal or plastic bands between the transducers that are designed to go over the top of the user's head. Newer designs are made to fit around the back of a user's neck, often with a clip that fits between the ears and head to minimize sliding. Some eschew the connection between transducers altogether and simply clip to each ear individually. Open and supra-aural headphones have padding that sits on a listener's ears. Usually this is removable and washable (and, when the time comes, replaceable).[20] Circumaural headphones sometimes use removable pads but more often use other materials that can be cleaned with a disinfectant.

In-ear headphones have become more commonplace in the past several years, thanks to the boom of portable audio devices. As with open headphones, they can be found with an over-the-head or behind-the-neck band, or without any band at all between the transducers. "Ear buds" are increasingly popular, which fit directly into the user's ear canals. Some ear buds are simply plastic, while others have removable pads or boots. If only for reasons of hygiene, the latter might be preferable for a library if extra pads can be purchased. From a practical standpoint, however, some pads tend to come off too easily and will eventually be lost.

Headphones are also defined by the kind of transducer used. The most common type is the moving coil, or dynamic, headphone. This design is basically a small conventional loudspeaker. These are very efficient and dependable, and, as the least expensive transducer for headphones, the kind most likely to be used in libraries. One difference among headphones, though, is the kind of magnet employed. In most designs, a simple ferrite magnet is used. Some designs are now using neodymium magnets. Neodymium, a rare earth element, makes a very strong magnetic field, which allows for less mass to be used to generate the same field strength. Using neodymium not only lightens the weight of traditional headphones, it has allowed headphone manufacturers to make the very small transducers employed in intra-aural headphones.

Like loudspeakers, though, other transducers are used for headphones as well. Isodynamic headphones are similar to small planar loudspeakers. Although lightweight, even when circumaural, they are inefficient and rarely can be driven by a typical headphone jack, requiring some kind of step-up device or separate amplifier that is usually sold together with the headphones. Electrostatic headphones can also be found and have similar characteristics as isodynamic phones. An even rarer variant of the electrostatic is the "electret transducer," which has a "permanently" polarized membrane that tends to depolarize with use and age. All three of these kinds of transducers share the same basic sonic characteristics of their full-sized loudspeaker cousins, which include very fast response and extraordinary detail, but they tend to be found only on expensive headphones.

There have been several attempts over the years to have headphones produce a convincing three-dimensional image. There are several reasons that this has been such an impossible task (especially before digital signal processing, or DSP), not the least of which is that the differences between people's ears play havoc with repeatable head-related transfer functions (HRTFs). Even small variations in ear geometry make it difficult to present the sounds arriving at precise times that let the brain interpret correctly spatial localization. Advances in DSP vis-à-vis multi-channel sound for home theater applications has found its way into headphone design as well, so that it is now possible for reasonable 3D sound to be approximated via stereo headphones. Indeed, the next big development in headphone usage will be the simulation of 5.1 or other multi-channel listening via stereo headphones. Several companies are working on Virtual Surround Sound technologies. For libraries that cannot set up home theater or surround sound listening environments and will require headphone listening for viewing DVDs, this is an exciting prospect.

Perhaps the most vexing aspect of headphone design, at least for libraries, is that almost no headphone today is terminated with a ¼-inch jack. Even the most expensive headphones are typically terminated with a mini-plug (⅛-inch, or 3.5 mm).[21] Only portable audio components or inexpensive mini-systems have a mini-plug headphone jack, however. Most non-portable audio components, if they have a headphone jack at all, use the standard ¼-inch socket, necessitating the use of a ⅛- to ¼-inch adaptor. What makes this problematic for libraries, of course, is that these adaptors are regularly stolen. There is no completely foolproof way of stopping theft of adapters. Various kinds of tape have been used, but no permanent solution has been found.[22]

Another frustrating aspect of headphone usage is their apparent fragility. Headphones seem to fail at a much more rapid rate than any other piece of equipment. Most frequently the problem occurs at one end of the cable or the other: where it's connected to the earpieces, or at the plug. Sometimes the problem is not any part of the headphones, but the equipment jack into which the headphones are plugged. The problem usually takes the form of a channel that is missing or a "scratchiness" or "fuzzy" sound that occurs when the headphones are moved. If it is determined that the problem is where the cord connects to the earpiece, this is often caused because the cord is wrapped too tightly for storage. It is better not to wrap the cords at all, but where this is not possible care should be taken to minimize any tension at the point of contact between cable and earpiece.

Of course, cordless headphones would obviate this problem but might raise others. There are two varieties of cordless headphones: infrared and radio frequency. Both kinds have a base station into which the signal is fed, usually through an unbalanced, RCA-terminated, analog connection. Both kinds also require batteries (see the discussion in chapter 6 about batteries). Not all models have rechargeable batteries, but those that do require the phones to be locked into the base station or be connected to a recharger between uses. Infrared headphones require a line of sight from the phones to the base for the signal to work. Radio frequency headphones operate on the same principal as cordless telephones, transmitting an FM signal that allows the wearer to be up to several hundred feet away. In the United States today this is typically in the 900 MHz range, but other countries often specify different frequencies, and even in the United States the range used to be much lower. Cordless headphones only seem to come in circumaural or supra-aural styles. One of the most frequent complaints is that they become uncomfortable after wearing for a period of time because they tend to clamp to the user's head more forcefully than wired headphones.

FM-based wireless systems have a poor reputation for sound quality. They frequently suffer from a variety of interferences. Some of the better wireless headphones allow the user to change frequencies to find the best match for a given location. Libraries considering wireless phones should also assess the potential for interference among a number of cordless headphones in close proximity. Another possible concern is that of security since the headphones are not attached to anything. Perhaps the fact that they would not work without the base unit would be a deterrent.

The other place that traditional headphones, but typically not ear buds, can be easily broken is the earpiece itself. The coil, tightly wound copper wire held in place by shellac or a similar substance, can deform over time, especially when played loudly. Further, the diaphragm, or dome that is usually covered by felt or cloth, can be dented or broken from misuse. Both of these conditions will result in poor sound coming from that earpiece.

Professional-grade headphones tend to be more robust in their construction, and while initially more expensive may prove cost effective if they require less frequent repair or replacement. At the other end of the spectrum, purchasing very cheap headphones—knowing that they will not last—may make more financial sense as throwaways. It is also worth noting that Koss headphones have a lifetime guarantee. Some libraries take advantage of this and send broken headphones back to Koss for replacement.

## Focused Sound Installations

There have been several schemes that localize sound to a small physical space so that only one or a few listeners may hear, without disturbing others. They are found in museums, stores, cybercafes, and other places as an alternative to headphones. These schemes have included:

- Placing a tube around a driver to limit the area of coverage.
- A parabolic dome.
- A hemispheric dome.
- Heterodyne emitters.
- Steered speaker arrays, where the timing and angle of many identical drivers are carefully correlated to deliver sound to a particular point in space.[23]

Each of these methods has positives and negatives. For example, domes typically are suspended above a listener's head and focus the sound sources at the bowl of the dome, reflecting the sound to a point where the ears are expected to be. Hemispheric domes are deeper than parabolic domes and able to focus the sound more tightly.[24] However, as the sound becomes more focused to a specific point, the location of the listener's ears, within a few inches in the three-dimensional planes, becomes crucial. Heterodyne emitters focus their sound over only a few degrees but seem to have little musical application.

The only library of which I am aware that has installed sound domes is the Dallas Public Library, and the response has been negative.[25] Even though the claims are that 75-80% of the sound produced cannot be heard beyond the listener's position, there remains quite a bit of spillover, which may prove to be too much. Further, as would be expected from small speakers, their low frequency extension is not acceptable for music applications.[26]

## Notes

1. Readers who want a fully scientific explanation of engineering behind loudspeakers and headphones should consult John Borwick, ed., *Loudspeaker and Headphone Handbook*, 3rd ed. (Oxford: Focal Press, 2001).

2. The planar speaker is sometimes referred to as a ribbon speaker, although there is a technical difference between them. For more information refer to Harley, 210-15, and John Watkinson, "Transducer Drive Mechanisms," in Borwick, 44-107 passim.

3. It should be noted that the current enthusiasm for surround sound speakers has led to some very interesting speaker designs for wall-mounted speakers, some of which use planar technology. Where space is limited, these might be worth exploring.

4. For more detailed explanation, see Graham Bank and Julian Wright, "Loudspeaker Enclosures," in Borwick, 297-324.

5. The main difference between an acoustic suspension and an infinite baffle enclosure is that in the former, the air inside the speaker is part of the driver's suspension. The compliance of the air in the enclosure of an infinite baffle is greater than the compliance of the driver suspension, and in an acoustic suspension cabinet the compliance of the air is less. For more information see Gary Galo, "Loudspeakers: A Short History," *Speaker Builder* (June 1994): 19-21.

6. Isobarik is the trade name of a particular kind of speaker design by Linn Products. Employing a second driver behind the one facing out equalizes interior sound pressures, and effectively doubles the mass of the driver, thus lowering the front drivers' resonant frequency. This design ultimately allows for smaller enclosures with less transient distortion from the driver.

7. A.N. Thiele, "Loudspeakers in Vented Boxes, Parts 1 and 2," *Journal of the Audio Engineering Society* (May and June, 1971); Richard H. Small, "Vented-Box Loudspeaker Systems, Parts 1-4," *Journal of the Audio Engineering Society* (June, July/August, September, October 1973).

8. A common advertisement is for a satellite/subwoofer combination, that is, two small speakers and one subwoofer. Whether or not this is technically a subwoofer is debatable. The term "subwoofer" should refer to drivers that produce sound only in the lowest range, below 200 Hz. If that were the case in a sat/sub combination, then the small satellite speakers would be required to play well below where they are comfortable. Regardless, divorcing a woofer from the same cabinet that holds the mid- and/or upper-range drivers has some very positive benefits.

9. First order = 6 dB/octave, second order = 12 dB/octave, third order = 18 dB/octave, and fourth order = 24 dB/octave.

10. IEC standard 60268-5 (ed. 3.0, 2003) specifies measurement techniques and presentation of specifications. The AES also has a committee, SC-04-03 Working Group on Loudspeaker Modeling and Measurement, which is drafting a standard for loudspeaker measurement and specification.

11. For a good yet succinct discussion, see Harley, 246-54. For an attempt to correlate measurements to psycho-acoustics, see Mark F. Davis, "What's Really Important in Loudspeaker Performance?" *High Fidelity* (June 1978): 53-57. While Davis calls into question some measurable characteristics that various speaker makers still deem important, he at least attempts to justify his findings in terms of music reproduction in real world situations.

12. Watkinson, 98. Also Floyd E. Toole and Sean E. Olive discuss the difficulty of listening tests in "Subjective Evaluation," in Borwick, 565-84.

13. In the unlikely event that a library can make this adjustment, the reader is referred to Adams, 96-99 for a brief overview of the process, and Harley, 76-91 for a much more detailed discussion.

14. For an excellent discussion of room acoustics as they relate to loudspeakers, see Glyn Adams, "The Room Environment: Basic Theory," in Borwick, 325-74, and Philip Newell, "The Room Environment: Problems and Solutions," in Borwick, 375-410.

15. Martin Collums writes in "The Amplifier/Loudspeaker Interface," (in Borwick, 285) "Direct conversion from digital signals to sound pressure is the ultimate objective and may be possible with micro-machine pumps."

16. For a definition of these terms see C.A. Poldy, "Headphones," in Borwick, 586.

17. It should be noted that at least one company has attempted to overcome this issue. The RCA HP900 model headphones have a "vibration mode" (powered by a separate battery) that is supposed to simulate the visceral effect of subwoofers by means of a tactile transducer. Reviews indicate that the sound quality is poor, but that one's cranium is effectively rattled. These are marketed at the gaming and video (and perhaps hip-hop) markets.

18. Poldy, 663-64.

19. C.D. Mathers and K.F. Lansdowne, "Hearing Risk to Wearers of Circumaural Headphones: An Investigation," BBC Report RD 1979/3, quoted in Poldy, 657-58.

20. Most headphone cushions can be safely laundered in a washing machine on a gentle cycle in a mesh bag, and air-dried on a rack.

21. The better Grado headphones all terminate in a ¼-in jack. Their Prestige Series model SR-125, with a price under $150 (in 2005), tremendous build quality, and a very neutral sound is a great buy for libraries.

22. The Sibley Music Library uses the Checkpoint security system, which uses radio frequency tags instead of magnetic strips. These security tags have an extremely adhesive backing to prevent them from being easily removed from books. We use these tags to wrap around the adaptor and plug, and then wrap book tape around that. This has proved to be quite effective as a deterrent.

23. "Focused Sound," n.d., <http://www.dakotaaudio.com/pdf/whitepaper1.pdf> (November 13, 2004).

24. The principal manufacturer of sound domes seems to be Brown Innovations <www.browninnovations.com>.

25. Tina Murdock, "Re: [MLA-L] music library listening rooms," July 23, 2003, <MLA-L@LISTSERV.INDIANA.EDU>.

26. The Brown Innovations sound domes specify that they only extend to 150 Hz, or approximately D3. As another way of looking at it, the frequency response misses the lowest two-and-one-half octaves on a piano.

# CHAPTER 6

# MISCELLANEOUS

## Interconnects, Tweaks, Accessories, and Gadgets

Audiophiles may spend hours trying out various accessories and experiments in an effort to get everything sonically possible out of their system, even those with a modest price tag. Libraries are not going to do that, but some of the finer points of audio "tweaking" (as fine-tuning is called among audiophiles) are outlined below to which some consideration might be given. Audio accessories, especially the marketing of some of them, have given the hobby a bad name. It is true that some schemes simply are bogus, but some things that initially defy logic actually work. Sorting out the good from the bad is fun for many audiophiles, but drives others to distraction. In this chapter I discuss some of the things one reads about in audiophile literature and their applicability in libraries. Some may improve the audio experience of listeners, some are simply a matter of good maintenance, and others just do not make much sense in libraries.

### Cables and Speaker Wire

There are few audio products that engender such fierce debate as interconnects and speaker wire. In one camp are those that believe that wires and cables make absolutely no difference, indeed that it is *impossible* for there to be an audible variation between assorted kinds. As long as the connections are not broken, that should be good enough, and anyone who believes otherwise is deluding themselves into throwing away their money on snake oil. The other camp is populated by those who do hear a difference, and believe that proper cable matching is just as important as any other component one buys. Those who disagree are then tin-eared, by-the-specs-only types who cannot tell the difference between an oboe and a trumpet and are worthy only of scorn and derision. In this debate there is no middle ground. While I am firmly in the latter camp as an audiophile, I generally do not advocate that libraries worry much about interconnects. Interconnects are a way to fine-tune a system, but libraries would be better served buying superior equipment. High-end audiophiles can spend thousands of dollars just on interconnects, and speaker wire can sell for $250 per linear foot, but regardless of its quality, a cable cannot make up for any deficiencies in the rest of the hardware.[1]

The only exception would be the choice between a balanced and unbalanced analog connection between two components. Balanced is always preferable, but the choice almost never exists in the consumer-grade audio equipment most libraries buy. Almost all professional-level equipment uses balanced connections. Installations that have exceptionally long distances between components benefit the most from balanced connections. The reason for the difference is that balanced connections remove the possibility of electromagnetic disturbances, such as those from a nearby power cord. An unbalanced line has only two conductors, an inner (referenced to ground) and outer (screen). Balanced connections have a separate ground, in addition to two parallel conductors carrying the signal (180° out of phase with each other). When the signals reach their destination, a differential amplifier receives them and amplifies *only* the difference between the two signals, easily rejecting any noise that might have entered into the cable.

The only other caveats concerning interconnects are: keep them as short as possible, and clean their connections every year or two (more about which later). Even upgrading to the more modestly priced cables of aftermarket manufacturers should yield some improvements. If you decide to upgrade your cables, here are some things you should keep in mind. Be forewarned that the marketing schemes of some companies will make it seem as if their cables not only help your audio system but may lower your cholesterol. There are no specifications that are worthwhile for comparative purposes. The best advice, then, is to stick with a known cable manufacturer who also makes high-end cables, such as AudioQuest or Monster Cable, and buy an affordable model.

Analog interconnects, balanced or unbalanced, are made up of three parts: the conductors (the wires that electrically carry the signal), the insulating material around the conductors (referred to as the dielectric), and the terminations (the plugs that actually interface with the equipment). The type and quality of the metal used to make the conductors plays a large part in determining the price. High-end cable manufacturers tout the purity of the copper (you may see reference to "six nines" copper, which is 99.99997% pure), the structure of the copper's grains (LC, or Linear Crystal), and if it is Oxygen Free Copper (OFC). One of the selling points for some headphones is that their cords are made from OFC. Some interconnects even use silver instead of copper, to retard the oxidation and ultimate degradation of the metal.[2]

A cable's terminations are also important, regardless if one uses the "giveaway" interconnects that come with components or a more exotic set. First and foremost, the connection between cable and component *must* be tight. If the connection is loose, either the cable should be replaced or the jacks on the component should be fixed. One of the shortcomings of RCA plugs is that they do not lock into place, and over time become worn. At best a loose connection will result in poor sound quality, but usually it will result in an intermittent or broken signal. Some cables have an RCA plug that has a split center post, which works well providing that the jack into which it is inserted is small enough to squeeze the two sides together.

Better-quality terminations are gold plated.[3] Gold is a much better electrical conductor than the nickel plating used on giveaway cables. Further, gold inhibits oxidation that will naturally occur to metal. Terminations are typically soldered to the conductors. As ordinary solder is a terribly poor conductor, better cables use either a better grade solder (one with more silver content) or more of a welding technique to attach conductor to termination. Again, the goal is to allow a complex electrical signal to pass through as unscathed as possible, and even the less expensive after-market cables are more likely to allow this to take place than cheap throwaways.

The dielectric material can be of some importance to the sound quality of a given cable, but will probably never realistically come into play in a library's purchasing decision. Nevertheless, one should know that the material surrounding the conductors will absorb some energy, which can then be transmitted at a slightly delayed time. Only in a vacuum would dielectric absorption not take place. High-end cable manufacturers have tried many materials to reduce this effect, but the cables that a library will buy will have PVC or some kind of plastic.[4]

The most critical cabling in an audio system is between an amplifier and speaker. Interconnects carry relatively low-level signals in comparison to speaker cables. Speaker wires vary in resistance, and this resistance affects how much control an amplifier has over the speaker, especially in low frequencies. As the speaker wire lengthens, its resistance increases and power is lost in the low-impedance speaker circuit, which is the main reason to keep speaker wire runs as short as possible.[5] Unlike interconnects, speaker cables can be terminated in a variety of ways (or simply left bare) that all connect to the same five-way binding posts. The most common connectors are spade lugs and banana connectors. Spade lugs (shaped like half-circles) are designed to encircle the binding post, banana connectors to go into the hole in the middle of the binding post. If connections are eschewed in favor of bare wire, the wire should go straight into the hole of the binding post and tightened, not wrapped around the outside. This is not a bad choice if the terminations are soldered to the wire instead of crimped or welded.

As mentioned above in the section about preamplifiers, there are different kinds of digital connections between components. One might think that the kind of digital cable—optical or coaxial—should not matter, as it is just carrying a stream of ones and zeros from one point to another. However, it does seem to matter. Jitter, the timing errors that occur getting a digital signal from one point to another, seems to be worse in most optical cables. Why this should be is still debated. Certainly there are different grades of optical cable, with better cables having a wider bandwidth and better light-conducting properties due to their advanced materials. The TosLink connection is widely dismissed for its poor audio performance; digital connections are best made with coax.[6] Further, true 75 Ω RCA or BNC connectors are preferred, although few components are made that utilize the BNC connection.

Regardless if one uses cables supplied with equipment or after-market wire, there are certain housekeeping issues that should be observed. First, try to keep AC power cords as far away as possible from interconnects and speaker wire, and certainly do not tie them all together for appearance's sake! It is especially crucial to keep power cords away from phono leads. One of the first things a technician does when trying to diagnose hum in a system is check whether a power cord is lying next to an audio cable. Consideration might be given to the location of each piece of equipment to minimize tangled cables. If they cannot be completely separated, they should be made to cross at right angles to reduce the amount of contact, and it is even better to put space between them with a small block of wood, Styrofoam, or any other inert material.

While it is always worthwhile to use the shortest lengths of cables possible, if one does have a length too long, avoid the temptation to "neaten things up" by creating a tidy loop, which often creates a very effective antenna for unwanted signals. Cables should not be bent. Disconnect and clean each cable and speaker connection every year or two. Oxidation naturally occurs to metal over time, which an electrical contact cleaner, such as Kontak or CAIG Pro Gold, can remove easily. Cables should never be disconnected by pulling on the cable proper, but by grasping only the plug.

**Other Ways to Improve Sound**

As mentioned in the first chapter, some care should be given towards the quality of the AC power upon which the equipment feeds. When replacing equipment in an existing room or system, it may not be possible to do anything with the basic power supply. Electromagnetic noise can be generated from a number of sources, though, and even clean power at the AC outlet might not eliminate every problem. The components themselves, or perhaps just one, might have a problem. In these cases an AC power conditioner could be a solution. More than just a power strip[7] or surge protector, these are active devices that work towards ridding a system of EMI and RFI, sending clean 60 Hz AC power to each component. AC line conditioners generally are overkill in most library settings, but it is important that each component be plugged into its own power outlet. Using the power plugs that are present on the backs of some components is not a wise decision if it can be avoided. If the system is experiencing a problem only with RFI, RF filters (or "chokes") on interconnects and power cords are an inexpensive solution.

In systems that use power amplifiers and loudspeakers, the amp is best served if plugged into its own AC outlet on its own circuit, although in buildings such as libraries this is an unlikely possibility. The reason for this approach is the way that power amps draw current. Unlike source components that draw a fairly constant and relatively small amount of power, push-pull amplifiers draw more or less power to drive the speakers as the music demands.

Turntables have long been a tweaker's playground. Taking a basic turntable system and making it sound much better than when it came from the manufacturer is many an audiophile's dream. While libraries almost never are in the business of serious tweaking, there are some considerations for turntables in particular that might be useful.

A turntable takes mechanical energy in the form of vibrations and converts it to electrical energy. However, the turntable system has no way of knowing if the vibrations are those desired by virtue of their existence in the grooves of the record, or if the vibrations are coming from another source. If one can determine origins of the unwanted vibrations, measures can be taken to eliminate or reduce them. For example, if the vibrations are noticeable when someone is walking past the audio system, then it is likely that the turntable is not isolated enough from its surroundings. Isolation stands are typically too expensive—and awkward in a library situation—but there are various kinds of feet that can be used to decouple the turntable from the surface on which it sits. Most of these are fairly inexpensive. Some are inverted cones, where only a point touches the surface, while others are made out of inert material such as sorbothane to absorb vibrations before they reach the feet of the turntable proper. Unfortunately, most of these isolation techniques run contrary to theft-prevention measures.

There might also be vibrations induced by the turntable itself that enter into the record from the platter/mat below. This is fairly common with direct-drive turntables. Inexpensive models that have very light platters often produce a distinct low frequency rumble. Platter mats made out of sorbothane or similar materials can greatly dampen these kinds of internal vibrations, especially when used in conjunction with a record clamp, although clamps are not practical where users play their own recordings.[8] Vacuum hold-down systems, though excellent, are both expensive and not practical for library use.

An often overlooked aspect of good sound, when loudspeakers are used, is proper room setup. A typical listening room with speakers can be an acoustic nightmare. Even if the equipment is well selected, the interactions between the speakers and space can destroy any semblance of good sound. It is important, then, in this kind of environment to give some thought to various acoustic treatments that can tame the problems one might experience. Since most libraries do not use speakers, and where they are used often there is little that can be done about where speakers are placed, the point will not be belabored here. An excellent discussion of room design and the various products that can help can be found in Robert Harley's *The Complete Guide to High-End Audio*.[9]

As mentioned at the outset of this section, there are many accessories and modifications sold to audiophiles that are of dubious distinction or that simply are not appropriate or useful in libraries. Librarians who are not audiophiles themselves, but who may rely on the advice of an associate who is, may hear of some of the following suggestions:

- Cartridge demagnetizers plug into your turntable's output cables, and when turned on help remove built-up residual magnetism in the cartridge. They are sometimes referred to as "fluxbusters" after the first model was introduced in the 1980s by Sumiko by that name. They are most useful for systems with MC cartridges, which libraries rarely have. Using one with a MM cartridge is more difficult because the stylus must be removed first. A cartridge demagnetizer probably can be ignored by most libraries.

- Shorting plugs or RCA Caps are made to be inserted into unused RCA jacks on any component. There was a time when preamplifiers were shipped with them because airborne RFI and EMI were more problematic. Newer designs have more or less obviated the need for them, however. Note that shorting plugs are only for use on inputs, although caps can be used on any female RCA plug.

- Interconnects and speaker wires change subtly over their first hours of service. Cable enhancers "break in" new cables so that they are at their optimum performance when placed into a system. Breaking in cables is not likely to make much difference at the price points at which libraries buy.

- After-market power cords are popular among high-end audiophiles, replacing the stock cords that come with a piece of equipment. A library's budget is probably better spent elsewhere than on upgraded power cords.

## Circulating Equipment

The first chapter explored some of the pros and cons of circulating portable audio and video equipment. This section surveys the possibilities.

In these days of iPods, PDAs, and even handheld DVD players, it is striking to note that the Sony Walkman model TPS-L2, with a list price of $199.95, first came to market in July 1979. Handheld AM radios became commonplace beginning in the 1960s, but the Walkman portable tape player became an icon that has reshaped the audio industry in the last quarter-century. As Xerox is to photocopying, the word "walkman" is now the generic name for all such personal audio and video equipment.

Libraries have been slow to embrace portable technology. Whether it is a concern for lost or damaged equipment, possible concerns about audio quality, a general disdain towards the cassette medium, an "it's-never-been-done-this-way" attitude, or other forces at work, the walkman lifestyle has not made an impact in libraries. Even the introduction of the Discman in 1986, which allowed listening to "indestructible" CDs anywhere in the library, did not usher in a new era of listening possibilities. Portable video devices have been slow to gain acceptance, even in the consumer market. Those libraries that are now using or planning to use circulating equipment have many options.

**General Considerations**

A certain segment of the portable market is geared towards those who listen while they engage in some physical activity such as running, biking, or working out at a gym. Often these players are heat- and moisture-resistant and generally are better built to withstand the rigors and abuse they take from this kind of use. This makes them ideal candidates for library usage. Some more expensive models employ a metal body (usually aluminum or magnesium), which further limits the amount of damage that can be inflicted by careless usage. Indeed, a unit's hardiness is perhaps of more overriding concern than sound quality. Some of that better build quality (e.g. a sturdier headphone circuit) translates into better sounding equipment.

One of the principal concerns of circulating portable equipment is about power. All are designed to be run on batteries, but some models come with an AC adapter to save battery life. If the adapter is used, then the unit and user are tethered to a wall outlet. One very useful feature that some models have is an automatic shutoff after a period of non-use. Batteries need careful consideration for a few reasons, though. First, you must determine which kind to use. Standard carbon batteries should be avoided because they wear out so quickly in this kind of application. Alkaline batteries provide the most hours of operation before replacement is necessary but are disposable.[10] How often they need replacement is, of course, determined by how much usage the equipment receives. Further, alkaline batteries are considered hazardous waste in many areas, and may require special handling for disposal. Some portable equipment, primarily digital music players, operates on only one battery, which might be a significant factor in the purchasing decision.

Rechargeable batteries might be an attractive option because they are not as disposable and can save considerable money over time, but there are several issues to cons99ider. First, even rechargeable batteries will not hold their power after a certain number of charges, so these are not batteries for life. Second, rechargeable batteries do not have the power capacity of alkalines, nor do they have the same power output (1.25 V for a AA cell, compared to an alkaline battery's 1.5 V). Equipment such as a portable CD player can drain rechargeable batteries fairly quickly. Third, how and when to recharge them must be considered. Only the most expensive portables have a recharging dock or stand, which means that the batteries will likely need to be removed from the player to recharge. Most models have their battery compartment on the outside; some, including many of the sport models, have the compartment inside where the CD is loaded. Not only does this make changing batteries somewhat awkward, but greatly increases the risk of damage to the laser assembly and other delicate parts. Also worth noting is that some digital music players do not have a user-replaceable battery at all, requiring a service center to do that. This not only makes replacing batteries inconvenient, but potentially expensive.

When to change the batteries is also of concern, especially those made of nickel cadmium (NiCd or Nicad). Most batteries last longer if they are discharged fully before recharging, due to a "memory effect." This means that if a battery is only half discharged before recharging, in time that is about as far as it will recharge in the future, thus limiting its life. Nicad batteries are the oldest kind of rechargeable battery and suffer most from this memory effect. Cadmium is also a very toxic chemical. Newer technologies—Nickel Metal Hydride (NiMH) and Lithium Ion (Li-Ion)—suffer less from memory effect, but are significantly more expensive. The kind of battery charger should also be carefully chosen. So-called "intelligent" rechargers turn off after the batteries are fully charged,[11] whereas most simple rechargers can overcharge and thus damage batteries. The expense of batteries also brings up the concern for security. Since many users themselves have battery-operated equipment, expensive rechargeable—or just new—batteries might be tempting to swap for their used alkaline batteries.

Directly related to battery life is the one specification that is noteworthy when provided: a player's power output. Better players usually have 40+ mW/channel at 16 $\Omega$, whereas most are in the 20 mW range. More power output means that the batteries will not last as long, but usually means that at least some attention has been given to sound quality, especially at higher volume levels. Just as with power amplifiers driving loudspeakers, too little power output will cause significant distortion at all but the lowest volume levels.

"Volume limiting" (AVLS or Automatic Volume Limiter System) is a term coined by Sony. It refers to a volume control feature on some portable audio equipment. AVLS manages the audio signal and automatically decreases it if the volume rises above a prescribed level, or brings it up if the audio becomes too low. One advantage is that leakage from headphones is minimized, resulting in a quieter room environment. A second benefit is that suddenly loud sounds will not damage listeners' ears if they had the volume too high. Many of Sony's products that use this technology have two different level presets. One "feature" that seems ubiquitous among all portables is some kind of "bass boost" button that artificially increases some amount of the bass range. Similar to a loudness button found on some preamplifiers, it will be up to the individual user whether or not to use it.

The weakest point on any portable player is the junction between the headphone and player. Most often the problem is unfortunately not with the headphones—which could be replaced—but with the jack itself. Sometimes the contacts become corroded, but more often than not the points where the jack is soldered or otherwise connected to the circuit board break down. The results are "fuzzy" or "static-y" sound and intermittent dropouts, especially when the headphone plug is moved. Even the reputation of the vaunted iPod Mini has suffered because so many people have had this difficulty, the result of substandard construction. The parts density in portables is such that repairing broken solder joints is almost impossible, and the unit must be discarded.

**Portable CD Players**

Even at their most expensive, portable CD players are under $200, and there are several models under $40. Almost all of them are very compact in design (slightly larger in diameter than a CD), fairly lightweight, and often have pretty good sound.[12] Virtually all of them come with headphones and some kind of LCD readout or display. The displays may vary in the amount of information provided, though. Some provide just minimal information such as the track number and the elapsed time. Better models will also allow the user to see other kinds of information, including total time, total time remaining, track time remaining, track titles if the disc is so encoded, and so forth. Some models also include a backlit display, which is very helpful in darkened environments, and the most expensive models can have a color LCD display. Some models also include MP3 playback capability, although not from some internal memory, but rather from CD-Rs (or CD-RWs) with MP3s burned on them.

Another consideration is the buttons and controls. In an effort to make players as small as possible, manufacturers sometimes reduce the size of the buttons to the point where it is difficult to operate the player. Also note the legends on the buttons. Are they convenient and easy to understand? Are they only silk-screened on the buttons, which will be worn off, or does the button have a physical impression of the function? The latter obviously is more desirable. Some models have buttons not only on the outside, but also in the compartment where the disc spins. Often these buttons are for little-used options such as bass boost but are inconvenient nonetheless.

Some portables are now coming with remote control, either built into the headphone cord or as a separate handheld unit. A remote may simply substitute for or eliminate the controls on the player itself, or may include expanded functionality that would otherwise be missing.

However, since it is not permanently attached to the player, it becomes a third piece of the unit—together with the player and headphones—of which to keep track.

One of the most important features of a portable CD player is skip protection, which is the ability of the player to avoid interruption of the sound due to it being jostled or moved. Manufacturers have different names for this feature: Sony has used Steadysound or G-Protection, Aiwa's name is EASS (Electronic Anti-Shock System), Panasonic has used Anti-Shock Memory, and so forth. This is typically accomplished by using a memory chip to store a certain length of audio: between 20 and 80 seconds, depending on the model. When an interruption in the datastream occurs, the chip sends the buffered signal to the headphones and reconstructs the data once normal playback is restored. The downside to this technology is that using it puts a significant drain on the battery. Reviews of portable CD players indicate that some are better than others when it comes to maintaining a steady stream of sound.

Many of the better models come with some kind of lock or hold function. When set, buttons that are accidentally pushed do nothing. On some models this includes the volume controls, but on others the volume is unaffected by this feature. Most portable models come with features that seem unimportant, or useful only for certain applications. For example, track programming (the ability to make a CD play in a particular order instead of from beginning to end) may not be generally useful to everyone. Various other kinds of playback modes—such as random play, repeat disc, and repeat track—may be similarly inconsequential. Many portable CD players also come with a built-in AM/FM radio tuner. Unless providing radio content to your users is important, this becomes an option to avoid. Of two similarly priced models, one with and one without a built-in radio, the former will have compromises that the latter may not, especially in construction quality. All things being equal, opting for the simpler unit is usually better.

One feature that may or may not be important to a library is a player's compatibility. Virtually all portable players made today will play both CD and CD-R discs. Many will also play MP3-encoded discs as well. Not all will play CD-RW discs, though.

## Cassette Players

Many of the same issues regarding portable CD players equate to cassette players: unnecessary options such as a radio tuner, remote control, battery options, display readouts, etc. Indeed, it is difficult to find portable cassette players, except the very cheapest, that do not incorporate an AM/FM tuner, and often a TV or weather tuner as well. While in and of itself a tuner is not problematic, listening to the radio may not be the purpose for which a library purchased this kind of equipment. There are a few issues unique to cassettes though. Many portable cassette players also have the ability to record, often with a built-in microphone. This, too, may not be problematic. Unlike stationary cassette decks, most portables do not have a line input that might encourage recording directly from disc, but this is a feature that may not be germane to the unit's anticipated usage. Another frequent "feature" that would likely not fit with library usage is a built-in speaker. The desirability of a small speaker in the privacy of one's home is logical but seems impractical in the confines of a library.

There are some useful features to consider. Many portable cassette players, notably those made by Sony, have an "anti-rolling mechanism," which is designed to maintain a smooth tape transport across the playback head even when the unit is jostled (as when walking). Some portable cassette players also have an auto-reverse function, which plays the second side of a tape automatically without user intervention. As noted above, auto-reverse cassette decks are not without their sonic problems due to the impossibility of proper azimuth adjustment. On the other hand, cassettes are a low-fidelity medium, and perhaps do not merit as much attention given to them for their sonic characteristics.

Not all portable cassette players drain battery power at the same rate. Some players only require one AA battery, but most require two or come with a rechargeable battery. Claims of 30 or more hours of continuous tape play are not uncommon. Another difference between portable players and stand-alone decks is that the former rarely include Dolby noise reduction. Only some of the most expensive portables offer this. As a result, tapes encoded with Dolby B or C will sound unusually bright or harsh. Further, portable cassette players almost never allow the user to change the tape type (e.g. normal bias or $CrO_2$), further limiting the player's ability to accurately play back a given tape.

## Digital Music Players

In 2004, Duke University began to issue a new Apple iPod to all incoming freshman, ostensibly not only for entertainment purposes but with the idea that several legitimate educational uses are possible. The iPods will be loaded with Duke-related content, and students will also be able to download course materials or purchase individual songs as well.[13] Although I am unaware of any library that has yet added digital music players as a way of circulating music (e.g. reserve listening), this seems a logical step.[14] Duke upperclassmen who do not have iPods and who enroll in classes making use of the iPod experiment will be given loaners for the duration of the course.

Digital music players are often referred to as "MP3 players" even though most can play more than just the MP3 file format. One of their great advantages over portable CD or cassette players is the lack of moving parts. Most of the design is done with circuits and chips, which should result in a device much less prone to failures (certainly with less that can go wrong). Some digital music players have small internal hard drives, which would, after the connection between player and headphone, be the part most likely to fail. By incorporating a hard drive, though, the player's internal memory can go from megabytes to gigabytes. Hard drive-based players tend to be larger and heavier than flash-memory players, although new to the market are models such as the iPod Mini that have a more modest-sized hard drive (1-4 GB capacity, sometimes referred to as micro-drives) that are almost as light as the flash players. Indeed, in 2004 iRiver announced "necklace" style of digital music player that weighs only three-quarters of an ounce but has up to 512 MB of storage capacity.

The amount of internal memory available is one of the most significant differences between players. The compression scheme of MP3 audio (at 128 KB/s) is approximately 10:1, so that one minute of two-channel MP3 sound occupies about 1 MB of memory. Most players, especially those without a hard drive, also offer some kind of removable media (Memory Stick, CompactFlash, SmartMedia, Secure Digital, and MMC are the most common flash memory cards). Beyond music files, digital music players can now store text, video, images, and other digital files. If the legal issues are not insurmountable, one way for libraries to apply such technology is to encode memory cards with course reserves to circulate with players.

The current generation of digital music players can store and play a variety of digital music formats. If a library is using a format other than MP3, then, it is important to ensure the compatibility of the players. Among the other formats supported by various players are:

- WMA (Windows Media Audio, of which there are two kinds—secure and not—and often the former is not supported)
- RAM (RealAudio)
- AAC (Advanced Audio Coding, used for all iPods)
- AUD (Audible, designed for spoken word and audiobooks)
- WAV (uncompressed audio)
- AIFF (Audio Interchange File Format, Apple's proprietary uncompressed audio)

- Ogg Vorbis (an open source codec that arguably offers the best sound of any compressed format)
- ASF (Advanced Systems Format, also referred to by its earlier name Advanced Streaming Format, a multimedia file format for Windows Media)
- FLAC (Free Lossless Audio Codec)
- VBR (Variable Bit Rate)

The iRiver and Rio players are particularly flexible in this respect. Some of the better digital music players are also upgradeable, so that, as future formats are released, the player does not become obsolete. It is beyond the scope of this book to go into detail about these various music formats.

In addition to file compatibility, another important issue is computer compatibility. All digital music players are designed to connect to a computer so that content can be downloaded. This usually means that software must be installed on the computer that will allow the computer to recognize the player and its memory. Some models plug in and are recognized by the computer as an external drive, allowing one to drag-and-drop files. Some digital music players are only PC compatible (for example, the Creative Labs Xen line of players), and, further, only with very recent operating systems (the iPod for example will only work with Microsoft Windows 2000 and XP). This means one cannot successfully squeeze a few more months or years out of an older PC by using it to encode digital music players. Another compatibility issue may be the connection between player and computer. Most players support USB (Universal Serial Bus) connections, but some do not support the older USB 1.1 standard. Other types of connections include serial port, which is much slower than USB, and FireWire (also known as IEEE-1394, initially an Apple product that is even faster than USB).

Another item to consider with digital music players is the display. As with portable CD players, what and how each unit displays information is different. Something that may be important for library use is the recognition of ID3 tags, the metadata for each track that can give a wealth of information.[15] In order to make good use of this information, attention must be given to the number of lines of display, the size of the display, and the visual quality of the readout (e.g. backlit). Some screens also seem to be more easily scratched. Beyond reading the display, how the user navigates is also easier on some models than on others. It is also worth noting that if a library is intending to circulate players loaded with tracks in a certain listening order, referred to as the "playlist," this can often be changed by the user. Some models allow the user to "rate" the tracks (always referred to in the literature as "songs"), which makes higher-rated tracks play more frequently.

Reviews of digital music players tend to be found more in computer and tech-related journals and websites than audio, underscoring the close relationship between players and the computer world.[16] Still it is worthwhile to check on any piece of equipment before investing. For example, some models exhibit a long pause between tracks. Other models use more battery power, requiring more frequent charging. Little of use is said about the audio quality of the players, which does vary. The DACs used, for example, are almost never discussed. Given the ubiquity of the MP3 format over better-sounding compression schemes, perhaps this is not of greatest importance. However, some models do attempt to provide more sonic quality than others, typically those that support file formats such as FLAC or Ogg Vorbis. These are worth searching out.

## Portable Video Players

Portable video may never occupy a significant part of the market, certainly not the way audio components have. The way people listen to music versus the way they watch video speaks to this. One of the biggest selling points of portable audio players is that one can be doing other activities—exercising, working, etc.—while using the device. Watching a movie occupies more of one's senses. Further, a small screen will never convey the same impact that even a television can. Nevertheless, many library viewing setups, especially in carrels, are already on small screens (compared to what people are used to in their homes), so perhaps portable video will find some applicability in libraries.

Portable DVD players seem to have found some favor among consumers. Prices have dropped dramatically, and it is now possible to buy one for about $150. The price structure for portable DVDs is tied directly to screen size. What to look for in a portable DVD player is much like what is described in chapter 3 concerning full-sized DVD players (surround decoders, 3:2 pulldown, etc.) and video screens (resolution, number of pixels, etc.), combined with the issues facing portable audio components noted above (battery life, shock resistance, etc.). To date no portable DVD player is "blu-ray" compatible, although that will likely change by 2006. Portable DVD players incorporate some features worth considering, including:

- Multiple headphone jacks.

- The ability to play different formats, including DVD-A, DVD-R, DVD-RAM, CD, video CD, MP3, WMA, etc.
- Virtual Surround Sound, DSP-based surround sound decoding designed to simulate multi-channel sound through headphones.

Beyond portable DVDs, the industry is experimenting with portable DVRs, sometimes referred to as Personal Video Players (PVP), Portable Media Centers (PMC), or Portable Media Players (PMP). Based on the same principles as digital music players, these devices, typically much smaller than portable DVDs, play digital video files in a variety of formats. There are several inherent problems with this technology at present, some of which make the applicability of such devices in libraries questionable. Video files are significantly larger than audio files, and relatively few consumers maintain a library of movies on their computers. Many PVPs are designed to be connected to a consumer's cable or satellite box, from which content would be downloaded. PVPs have very small screen sizes, all less than 4 in. Commuters who want to catch up on missed sitcoms or sporting events may be satisfied, but viewing a full opera would be taxing. Compatibility with non-video file formats is rarely a problem, however: with their enormous storage capacity, PVPs can carry hundreds if not thousands of audio tracks, and display still images as well. Players either use small hard discs for storage or flash memory.

### Headphones

While every portable comes with a set of headphones, the connection between them is the single weakest link in the audio chain. When something begins to go wrong with the sound, it is often where the headphone plugs into the piece of equipment. If the problem is not there, then where the headphone cord connects to the headphones proper will be the breakdown point. The "earbud" style, however, seems to be less prone to this kind of problem. At that point, headphones for portables are cheaper to replace than fix. There are several style options, described above in the section on headphones.

## Computers as Audio Equipment

Dependency on a particular physical carrier (e.g., cassette, LP, CD) is becoming increasingly irrelevant, and we must now face audio recordings simply being digital files. In order to properly organize, display, and listen to these files, computers become the primary piece of equipment necessary to carry out this task, taking on the roles of source component and amplification/electronics. We still require either headphones or loudspeakers, but of the latter, the typical computer-grade speakers are woefully inadequate for a satisfactory listening experience.

What decisions need to be made regarding an adequate computer for listening to music? For the purposes of this discussion, the assumption will be made that the computers in question will not be used as a typical consumer computer would be, that is, without the ability to rip or record CDs. How the files are delivered to this computer is also beyond the scope of this discussion. On the whole, any computer with a sound card and the right software can do the job. Nevertheless there are some issues worth considering for using computers to deliver audio.

The presentation of multimedia files has always been one of the main fuel cells in the heated battle between PCs and Apple. If one's institution is solidly Mac or solidly PC, this is a moot point since one will not have a choice of platform. Despite the reputation of Macintosh being a better machine for multimedia uses, Macs are limited by the availability of software to perform various functions. If the Macintosh has the necessary functionality you require, then this relative inflexibility may not matter. The bundling that Apple does with its software might even be seen as a plus. If using a Mac for audio-only purposes were to be the only implementation of Macs in a library, then having one's users learn the differences in basic operations just for this one purpose might be questionable.

If one will be using PCs, the question of which Windows operating system to use comes into question. Windows 95 and 98 can be adequate, if minimal, operating systems. However, Windows 2000 and XP offer significant improvements in resource handling and memory allocation. Windows XP, though, incorporates SAP (Secure Audio Path), a piece of software built into Windows XP that works with or without Microsoft's DRM (Digital Rights Management) to thwart unauthorized media copying. Although SAP and DRM do not, at the moment, seem to be affecting negatively any applications that libraries are implementing, the possibility remains. It should be noted that Microsoft is making plans for improving audio quality with its Universal Audio Architecture initiative. Indeed, Microsoft has been collaborating with industry leader Intel to provide High Definition Audio chips and drivers.[17]

The one fact of life with any computer is that one can never have enough memory, not on a hard drive and not in RAM. Current operating systems occupy a lot of internal resources, and are not likely to diminish in space or needs. The issues of using a computer for audio or video magnify the need for increased memory. Uncompressed stereo

audio files can take up to 10 MB per minute, and 128 KB/s MP3s occupy about 1 MB per minute. Video, even compressed, takes up significantly more disk space. If the computers you will be using for audio
will only be for streaming, not storing individual files, then your needs
for large hard drives are significantly lessened.

Sound cards are potentially a significant issue. Virtually any sound
card will play MP3s or audio CDs, and more are beginning to support
DVD-A, but there are differences both in audio quality and flexibility
of features. Since MP3s are a compressed sound file anyway, perhaps it
is less important to make available a quality sound card if the primary
task of the machine will be for listening to streamed audio. Nevertheless, using a high-quality, after-market soundcard is one way to offer a
better listening experience. IT professionals, however, do not necessarily see any advantages. Most after-market sound cards are aimed at
either computer gamers or professional audio uses, making it difficult
to find useful product reviews. Further, most consumer-grade, after-
market cards are multi-channel (at least 5.1, and many now are 7.1),
and unless a library is supporting surround sound applications, these
kinds of sound cards are overkill. Cards for the gaming market often
have technology that is unimportant for music or video, such as
DirectX or EAX (a special effects audio suite). These are not inherently
bad, but can cause confusion to the buyer.

Nevertheless, when searching for computers for audio playback
(e.g., for streamed audio) there are some specifications to bear in mind,
if you can find them given by the manufacturer. In the case of an after-
market sound card, there are two kinds: internal and external. An external card makes little sense for a library installation, except that its controls can be placed within reach of the user. The controls for an internal
card will be handled virtually on the computer desktop. Internal cards
also come in two flavors, depending on the kind of slot or connection
(i.e. bus): PCI and ISA. Peripheral Component Interconnect (PCI) is the
better of the two options as it is faster. Industry Standard Architecture
(ISA) busses have largely been replaced by PCI but are sometimes included on new computers to allow slower devices to be connected. One
last item to consider is the compatibility of the card's drivers with the
operating system of the PC.

The technical specifications worth comparing are bit depth and
frequency, S/N ratio, and THD. Bit depth and frequency, usually expressed as 16 to 24 bits and 44.1 to 96 kHz, are the hallmark specs of
digital audio. As discussed in chapter 2, 16 bit 44.1 kHz is the red book
standard for CD audio, but many sound cards are only 8 bit. DVD-A
and other high quality digital formats will have larger bit depths and
higher frequency. A sound card that only specs out at 16/44.1 will not

be compatible with DVDs and may be of limited use. S/N (Signal-to-Noise) ratio is a more important specification than with stand-alone audio components because the interior of a computer is a potential minefield of noise that can get into the audio path. A S/N under 80 dB should be avoided, and those over 100 dB are preferred. THD (Total Harmonic Distortion) is perhaps the least important figure due to the different ways it can be measured and interpreted. THD can be measured at quite high levels in computers, with figures over 0.5% not infrequent. Better sound cards measure 0.05% or less.

As mentioned in chapter 1, using computers as a primary playback device for CDs is not recommended. However, most computers are equipped with some kind of disc drive. On the consumer market, these are often CD-R (or CD-RW) or DVD (and now DVD-R) drives. These kinds of recordable drives are often not suitable for general library usage as some will consider it an open opportunity to make unauthorized copies of material. The fact that most libraries have for decades provided publicly accessible photocopy machines where people can do the same thing seems to be overlooked in the debate about the appropriateness in libraries of sound *recording* equipment. Newer computers also have a plethora of high-speed ports—USB 2.0 or Firewire—into which consumers are expected to plug various gadgets, including digital music players or PDAs, which can be used to extract audio files stored on these computers.

A relatively recent piece of equipment introduced to the marketplace is the Digital Media Receiver, sometimes referred to as Digital Audio Receiver. This device takes server-based files and interfaces with a traditional stereo system. In the consumer market, realizing that PCs and home entertainment systems are often not in close proximity, DMRs are usually WiFi (802.11b) compatible; many also offer Ethernet connections. Some offer a built-in headphone jack, and all have analog and/or digital output connections. In libraries, such a device could eliminate the need for PCs devoted to listening. There are some caveats, however:

- Usually some kind of video device is required for programming, although an inexpensive monitor should suffice.
- As of this writing, most do not support Internet radio or subscription services (such as Rhapsody) unless explicitly stated.
- None support protected MP3 or AAC files (i.e. those files found at iTunes or Napster).
- Some offer very limited file-type support (although some, such as the Squeezebox by Slim Devices, support an impressive array of file types, including Ogg and FLAC).

- Most do not handle (or do so poorly) full motion video.
- Reviews of such devices have been mixed, primarily bemoaning their shortcomings while acknowledging that the concept is good.

There is some debate concerning how long such devices will be found as stand-alone units.[18] Already the technology is found in some DVD players. In time, this kind of convergence technology will be infused in all audio/video/computer equipment. When that day comes, not only will our patrons look blankly as we try to explain what an LP is and how to play it—on both sides—but they will also be confused by the quaint notion that there was a time when it took careful matching to make each piece of audio and video equipment work well together.

## Notes

1. Libraries that have technicians who can make cables have something of an advantage. A good choice, both sonically and fiscally, is D.H. Labs' BL-1 cable terminated with F-10 RCA plugs by Multicore SN62 solder, which is 2% silver content.

2. Collums describes various tests that have been done to gauge the effect of different copper qualities and crystalline structures on the resultant sound, 291-93.

3. Other, more expensive terminations are made from silver and even rhodium.

4. It has been suggested that a cable's dielectric will have more effect when used for digital audio transmission over long distances (see Allen Mornington-West, "Interconnections," in *Audio and Hi-Fi Handbook*, edited by Ian R. Sinclair, rev. 3rd ed. (Oxford: Newnes, 2000), 384.

5. Collums, 287.

6. There is another kind of digital connection and cable that provides superior jitter reduction: I2S. This is a five-conductor system that separates the word clock, the bit clock, and the master clock, developed by Philips as early as 1986. Although it is not a standard, a handful of high-end audio and video components have started to use I2S and I2S Enhanced (I2S*e*). It has yet to make an impact in the mass marketplace.

7. Power strips generally should be avoided if at all possible, as most of them are of poor construction. Instead of helping to eliminate noise, they are a likely culprit in the production of noise. There are a couple of well-made power strips that are designed for audio equipment made by Furman, Monster, and others. These usually include a built-in circuit breaker and RFI/EMI noise suppression. Whereas a cheap power strip can be bought for well under $10, better power strips start at $25.

8. A record clamp is a device that fits over the platter's spindle (while the record is on the platter) and presses down on the record to both flatten out modest warps and make the record as tight with the platter mat as possible.

9. "How to Get the Best Sound from Your Room," 75-123.

10. Some audiophiles also believe that they sound better than rechargeable batteries.

11. It has been suggested that only charging a battery to 80% or so of its maximum at least doubles the number of times it can be recharged. Determining when this point is reached, however, is not simple and requires vigilance.

12. Several years ago a Radio Shack portable CD player that cost well under $200 shook up the high-end audio market because it sounded so good.

13. "Duke to Give Apple iPods to First-Year Students for Educational Use," July 19, 2004, <http://www.dukenews.duke.edu/news/ipods_0704.html> (July 27, 2004).

14. As this book was going to press I discovered one institution, Baylor University, that had just started such a program. Twelve iPods can be checked out with the entire semester's reserve listening loaded on them.

15. While the encryption of ID3 tags for MP3 files is beyond the scope of this text, it is worth noting that ID3v2, at this point an informal standard, offers much hope in the realm of allowing for as much documentation as might be desired for a given file. Further, use of the Lyrics tag (now Lyrics3, which is actually part of the MP3 file and not a separate text file) will allow for more text (and images) to be associated with a file. The Lyrics tag does not seem to be supported yet by the portable community. See <http://www.id3.org/> for more information.

16. Compare, for example, any review from CNET.com (a worthy review site for most digital and computer-related items) with the review of the third generation iPod in *Stereophile* (by Wes Phillips, October 2003, vol. 26, no. 10, available at <http://www.stereophile.com/budgetcomponents/934/index.html>). In addition to the ergonomics and features that dominate other reviews, Phillips mentions who made the parts that went into the iPod (e.g. a Wolfson Microelectronics DAC) and emphasizes the sound quality.

17. "Microsoft's Universal Audio Architecture Initiative Gains Momentum," April 29, 2004, <http://www.eeproductcenter.com/showPressRelease.jhtml?articleID=X205630> (August 8, 2004). See also "Universal Audio Architecture (UAA) High Definition Audio Class Driver Available for Windows Server 2003, Windows XP, and Windows 2000," March 29, 2004, <http://support.micro-soft.com/default.aspx?scid=kb;en-us;835221> (August 8, 2004). Microsoft's UAA white paper may be downloaded at <http://www.microsoft.com/whdc/device/audio/uaa.mspx.>

18. Market research by the Diffusion Group suggests that DMRs will increase in sales through 2006, and then decrease sharply thereafter. See "Stand-Alone Digital Audio Receivers Face a Difficult Future," July 27, 2004, <http://biz.yahoo.com/iw/040727/070472.html> (August 8, 2004).

---

The audio industry, like librarians, loves acronyms and technical short-hand. This is not meant to be a comprehensive glossary of audio terms, but rather a list of abbreviations, acronyms, and technical terms found in this text. For more information, the reader should explore Guy Marco's *Encyclopedia of Recorded Sound in the United States* (Garland, 1993, with a revised edition to be published in 2004); J. Gordon Holt's *The Audio Glossary* (Audio Amateur Press, 1990, distributed by Old Colony Sound Laboratory); Glenn D. White's *The Audio Diction-ary* (2nd ed., University of Washington Press, 1991); J.M. Woodgate's "Terminology" in John Borwick's *Loudspeaker and Headphone Hand-book* (Focal Press, 2001, 700-10); "Glossary of Technical Terms" in Kenneth C. Pohlman's *Compact Disc Handbook*; Alan Cohen's *Audio Technology Fundamentals* (Howard W. Sams, 1989); the *Dictionary @ audiovideo101* (www.audiovideo101.com/dictionary/); the *Glossary of Home Theater Terms* (www.bus.ucf.edu/cwhite/theater/Glossary.htm); Deluxe Global Media Services' *Glossary* (www.disctronics.co.uk/ technology/glossary/glossary.htm); the *CD and DVD Glossary* (www. mscience.com/gloss.html); and AfterDawn.com's *Glossary* (www.af-terdawn.com/glossary/).

**5.1:** Common nomenclature for **Surround Sound** applications that use six speakers: front left, center, and right; rear left and right; and a **Subwoofer** (the latter being the ".1" since it is not a full-range speaker).

**6.1:** Similar to **5.1**, but adds a discreet rear center channel as well.

**AAC:** Advanced Audio Coding. An audio encoding method used by some companies for digital audio delivery. Compatible with wa-termarking and copy protection, the files are smaller than **MP3** but touted to be superior in sound quality. AAC can refer to either of two standards: **MPEG-2** AAC or MPEG-4 AAC (ISO/IEC 14496-3, Subpart 4). The former is often referred to as **MPEG-2** NBC (non-backwards-compatible).

**AC:** Alternating Current. A source of electricity where the direction of the current (from generator to source) is continually changing (in the United States, at 60 cycles/second). Direct current (**DC**) electricity does not cycle or reverse.

**AC3:** *See Dolby Digital.*

**Acoustic Suspension:** A kind of speaker cabinet that contains all acoustic energy inside.

**A/D:** Analog-to-Digital. Usually used to refer to the conversion of one to the other.

**ADAT:** Alesis Digital Audio Tape. A proprietary digital tape format developed by Alesis in 1993 for professional uses, it uses **S-VHS** tape onto which up to eight tracks of **CD**-quality digital audio can be recorded. ADAT II offers up to 20-bit resolution.

**AES:** Audio Engineering Society.

**AES/EBU:** Audio Engineering Society/European Broadcast Union. Agreed to a professional-grade format for transmitting digital audio data. *See S/PDIF.*

**AIFF:** Audio Interchange File Format. Apple's proprietary uncompressed audio codec.

**Anti-Skating (aka Bias, in British writings):** The force necessary to counteract the pull of a tonearm across a record's surface towards the center. Lack of anti-skating would result in the **Stylus** tracking hard on the inner groove wall, instead of riding in the middle of the groove.

**ASF:** Advanced Systems Format. Also referred to by its earlier name Advanced Streaming Format, a multi-media file format for Windows Media.

**ASV:** Audio Still Video. Still image files that can be found on some **DVD-A**s.

**ATRAC:** Adaptive Transform Acoustic Coding. A proprietary, 5:1 compression scheme invented by Sony for the **MiniDisc**.

**ATSC:** Advanced Television Systems Committee. The standard for **HDTV**.

**Audiophile:** (1) A person who appreciates and is often knowledgeable about good sound and the equipment to produce it, and who sees audio equipment as a means towards high-quality music reproduction in the home. (2) A fanatical zealot about audio equipment who spends countless hours adjusting and fussing with equipment, continually upgrading each piece in his system because he is never satisfied, and who is more interested in equipment than music.

**AVLS:** Automatic Volume Limiter System. A volume control invented by Sony and used on many of their portable models.

**A/V:** Audio/Visual (or Audio/Video). This usually refers to equipment designed for home theater use (e.g., an A/V receiver), or more broadly any application with both video and audio components.

**Azimuth:** Regarding magnetic tape, the angle of the head during playback measured against the straight edge of the tape. Ideally this should be 90°.

**Balanced/Unbalanced:** Refers to the kind of wiring between components. Balanced connections utilize two conductors and a grounded shield and are always found on professional equipment. Unbalanced connections, found typically on consumer-grade equipment, have a single wire and a grounded shield. Balanced wiring is superior for eliminating noise, especially over long distances.

**Bass Reflex:** An early kind of **Vented Loudspeaker**.

**Bi-Polar Transistor:** An amplifying semiconductor that uses two kinds of semiconducting material (one P and the other N) in the form of a sandwich.

**Bi-Radial Stylus.** *See Elliptical Stylus.*

**CAV:** Constant Angular Velocity. In a disc playback system, this means the speed of the disc is constant throughout playback. Thus, mechanically, this is a simpler design. Most Laserdiscs were made CAV (which is of course not compatible with **CLV**).

**CLV:** Constant Linear Velocity. In a disc playback system, this refers to a constantly changing speed of the disc throughout playback (slower on the outside tracks and faster as the pickup nears the center). The advantage to CLV is that the rate of data transfer is constant. All **CD**s and **DVD**s are CLV.

**CD:** Compact Disc. A registered trademark of both Sony and Philips.

**CD-I:** Compact Disc-Interactive. A **CD** that also incorporates graphics, text, video, and other data to present a multi-media experience.

**CD-R:** Compact Disc-Recordable. A one-time-only recordable **CD**.

**CD-RW:** Compact Disc-Recordable re-Writable. A recordable **CD** that can be erased and recorded onto many times.

**CES:** Consumer Electronics Show. A semiannual trade show where products are demonstrated for the press, distributors, and dealers, and new equipment is introduced.

**Channel:** The path of an electronic signal. **Stereo** is sometimes referred to as two channel, with the two channels (left and right) somewhat different. Note that if the same signal is sent to more than one speaker, it is still one channel, or monophonic.

**Clipping:** Severe distortion of the audio signal due to driving a device, especially an amplifier, beyond its rated level. Signal peaks are flattened, or clipped. Clipping can destroy **Drivers**, particularly tweeters.

**Composite Video:** A common video connection that combines a video signal's color information and brightness into one signal (*see also S-Video and Component Video*).

**Component video:** A video connection that separates a video signal into three parts—brightness and two color signals—yielding the most superior picture quality to date (*see also S-Video*).

**Compression, Digital:** Any method in which the file size of digital data is decreased. Lossy compression discards some of the data permanently; lossless compression allows for all of the data to be reassembled.

**Compression, Radio:** Radio often uses **Dynamic Range** compression to reduce the range from low to high volumes of sound, which allows a station to be heard over a larger area.

**CPPM:** Content Protection for Pre-Recorded Media. A 56-bit key copy protections system used on **DVD-A**s.

**CRT:** Cathode Ray Tube.

**D/A:** *See A/D.*

**DAC:** Digital-to-Analog Converter.

**DAR:** Digital Audio Receiver (*see DMR*)

**DASH:** Digital Audio Stationary Head. A digital audio recording unit that records digital signals to tape without using a rotary head (*see DAT*), much like an analog open reel machine.

**DAT:** Digital Audio Tape. A tape format for recording and storing digital signals. Early in its existence it was referred to as R-DAT because, like a **VCR**, the record and playback heads rotate.

**dB:** Abbreviation for decibel.

**dbx:** (1) A type of **Compression**/expansion noise reduction and dynamic range expansion for analog audio tape, incompatible with **Dolby Noise Reduction**. (2) A manufacturer specializing in signal processing and noise reduction equipment.

**DC:** Direct Current.

**DCC:** Digital Compact Cassette. A failed digital tape format.

**Dielectric:** The insulating material between two conductors, forming a capacitor.

**Dipole:** A loudspeaker system that radiates the full spectrum of sound from both the front and rear, such as a planar design.

**Direct Drive:** A kind of turntable where the motor turns at the same speed as the platter, and the spindle is the motor shaft.

**Distortion:** Any undesired change in or modification of an electrical or audio signal.

**DMR:** Digital Media Receiver. A piece of equipment that finds media files on networked computers and makes them available to home entertainment equipment such as TVs and stereos.

**Dolby Noise Reduction (Dolby NR):** A noise reduction system that records higher frequencies at an exaggerated level and during playback lowers those same frequencies to be in line with the rest of the signal. There are several varieties, including Dolby A (designed for professional applications and which targets four frequency bands), Dolby SR (a variation of Dolby A designed for movie production), and Dolby B and Dolby C (both for consumer cassettes).

**Dolby Digital:** Released in 1991, this was one of the first successful multi-**Channel** audio systems. It employs five discrete **Channels:** two speakers in front of the viewer (like standard **Stereo**), two in the rear, a center speaker, plus the ability to add Low Frequency Effects (LFE) through subwoofers. This became known in shorthand as "**5.1**" (the subwoofer effects being the ".1") and is also known as **AC-3** (Audio Code 3) or SR-D. Dolby, in conjunction with Lucasfilm, later added a rear center **Channel** and introduced **THX Surround EX**.

**Dolby HX, HX Pro:** Not a noise reduction system, but a bias adjustment to increase the high frequency range and improve the high frequency headroom of cassettes, while limiting distortions.

**Dolby Pro-Logic:** An analog, **Surround Sound** format that encodes four **Channels** onto two.

**Dolby Stereo:** The movie theater version of **Dolby Surround**.

**Dolby Surround:** The consumer version of **Dolby Stereo**, which encodes and decodes three-**Channel** (front left and right plus rear), analog surround from a **Stereo** presentation.

**Driver:** In a loudspeaker system or headphone, the individual components (transducers) that converts the electrical signal to sound waves. The most common types are domes (mid-range drivers and tweeters, or full-range drivers in headphones) or cones (woofer and mid-range drivers).

**DRM:** Digital Rights Management. A Microsoft "feature" built into its Windows operating system and MediaPlayer program to stem unauthorized duplication of copyrighted files.

**DSD:** Direct Stream Digital. An encoding scheme devised by Sony and Philips for use with the **SACD**.

**DSP:** Digital Signal Processor (or Processing). A chip in some A/V receivers or preamplifiers that alters the frequency and tonal balance of the signal, ostensibly to make the recording sound like it is in a jazz club, concert auditorium, rock stadium, or some other pre-defined acoustic space.

**DSS:** (1) Digital Speaker Systems. This kind of speaker accepts a digital input from a receiver/amplifier, or directly from a source component such as a **DVD**, and processes the signal internally before it is converted to an analog signal and reaches the **Drivers**. (2) Digital Satellite System. Audio and video source from satellites, sent to a dish receiver.

**DST:** Digital Stream Transfer. A lossless packing technique for storing **DSD**-encoded data onto discs.

**DTS:** Digital Theater Systems. A **Surround Sound** system competing with the various Dolby systems.

**DVD:** Digital Versatile Disc.

**DVD-A:** DVD-Audio. An audio-only disc format based on the **DVD** standard that offers higher quality audio than **CD**, plus the possibility of multi-channel playback.

**D-VHS:** As the acronym implies, a digital successor to **VHS**, but one that initially could only record digitally from satellite. It was announced in Japan in 1995, then to other countries three years later; pre-recorded D-VHS movies were introduced in 2002. Although visually superior to the first generations of **DVD**, with a minimal resolution of 1280x720, it never caught on in the marketplace.

**DVI:** Digital Visual (or Video) Interface. A standard for transmitting digital video; has three different specifications: DVI-D for digital signals, DVI-A for analog signals, and DVI-I for both (or integrated). This interface may be replaced by **HDMI**.

**Dynamic Range:** The ratio of the quietest to loudest sound level produced without distortion.

**EIA:** Electronic Industries Association.

**Elliptical Stylus:** A **Stylus** whose cross section in the plane of the disc surface is an ellipse. The footprints of an elliptical stylus are also elliptical.

**EMI:** Electro-Magnetic Interference.

**EQ:** Equalization, allows for the adjustment of sound by frequency band.

**Euroconnector:** *See SCART.*

**FET:** Field-Effect Transistor. A unipolar transistor that allows current to flow (as controlled by an electrostatic field) through a single-doped channel (P or N).

**Filter:** An electrical component or circuit that allows certain frequencies to pass, but not others. For example, a "high-pass filter" allows high frequencies to pass, but excludes lower frequencies. Filters can be active (incorporating amplification) or passive, gradual (or sloped) or "brick wall."

**Five-Way Binding Post:** A connector on an amplifier or loudspeaker that accepts the five most common ways to connect speaker wire: bare wire (either looped or straight through a hole), single conductor headphone tip (now obsolete), spade lug, or banana plug.

**FLAC:** Free Lossless Audio Codec. An ingenious, open source compression scheme that preserves all of the ones and zeros (hence the seemingly incongruent use of "lossless" and "codec" in the title).

**Frequency:** The measurement, in cycles per second, of a sound wave's oscillation. This is typically expressed in Hertz (Hz). A sound wave that vibrates 1000 times has a frequency of 1000 cycles/second, or 1000 (or 1 k) Hz. The range of frequencies that humans can typically hear is from 20 to 20,000 Hz, although many people can hear above and below those stated extremes.

**Gain:** An expression of the amount of amplification, usually expressed in decibels (**dB**).

**HDCD:** High Definition Compatible Digital. An encoding scheme to improve standard 16-bit/44.1 kHz **CD**s. Requires **CD** players with the HDCD decoding chip to realize full potential, but can be played on any **CD** or **DVD** player.

**HD-DVD:** (1) High-Density DVD. A format that provides for more data storage on a **DVD** disc. (2) High-Definition DVD. A higher resolution **DVD** format resulting in a better picture.

**HDMI:** High-Definition Multimedia Interface. A proposed standard to replace **DVI** for transmitting video signals, and can transmit uncompressed video and audio.

**HDTV:** High-Definition Television.

**H/DTV:** High-Definition Digital Television. Referring to the part of the **ATSC** standard for HD (as opposed to SD, or Standard Definition) digital broadcasts.

**HX-Pro:** *See Dolby HX.*

**Hyper-Elliptical Stylus:** A variation on the elliptical-shaped **Stylus** that allows more surface contact in the groove.

**IEC:** International Electrotechnical Commission. An international professional engineering organization that sets standards for electrotechnology.

**Integrated Amplifier:** A single piece of equipment that combines the functions of a preamplifer and power amplifier.

**Jitter:** Timing errors in the digital audio data stream, sometimes referred to as clock jitter or word clock jitter.

**KBs:** Referring to rate of data transfer, kilobits per second.

**LC:** Linear Crystal. Refers to the structure of copper's grains.

**LCD:** Liquid Crystal Display.

**LD:** Laserdisc.

**LFE:** Low Frequency Effects. The sound effects in movies that require **Subwoofers** to recreate, such as explosions.

**Line Contact Stylus:** A type of bi-radial (elliptical) **Stylus** which has long and narrow points of contact with the sides of the groove wall, more closely duplicating the vertical tracking angle of the cutting **Stylus**. This can be beneficial if there is an exact match with the **VTA** of the disc cutter, but this type of stylus is less forgiving of mismatches between recording and playback **VTA**.

**Linear Contact Stylus:** *See Line Contact Stylus.*

**Linear Tracking (LT, aka Tangential-Tracking):** A tonearm that moves in a direct line across the face of a record from outside to inside, as compared to a pivoting tonearm that moves in an arc-shaped line.

**Loading:** The various methods of providing the proper enclosure for the **Drivers** of a dynamic loudspeaker, particularly the woofer. It also refers to the "load" presented to an amplifier by a loudspeaker.

**LP:** Long-Playing record.

**LTA:** Linear Tracking Angle.

**MC:** Moving Coil phono cartridge.

**MicroLine Stylus:** *See Line Contact Stylus.*

**Microridge Stylus:** *See Line Contact Stylus.*

**MD (MiniDisc):** A digital disc recording format, now only supported by Sony.

**MDF:** Medium Density Fiberboard. A common dense, inert construction material for loudspeakers, used to minimize enclosure vibrations.

**MM:** Moving Magnet phono cartridge.

**MLP:** Meridian Lossless Packing. A lossless **Compression** technique developed by Meridian Audio for use with **DVD-A** discs. MLP is sometimes referred to as Packed PCM (**PPCM**) since it is based on **PCM** coding.

**Monoblocks:** Two matching, monophonic amplifiers designed to work in tandem, one for each speaker. These are exclusively the domain of very high-end audio, usually costing several thousand dollars per pair.

**MOSFET:** Metal Oxide Semiconductor Field Effect Transistor (*see FET*).

**MP3:** Shorthand for MPEG-1 Audio Layer III, an audio compression scheme developed in the 1990s by **MPEG**.

**MPEG:** Motion Picture Expert Group. A standards body that has developed several successful compression schemes.

**MPEG-2:** Standard encoding scheme for compressing video meant for high bandwidth or broadband applications.

**MPX Filter:** A switch on many cassette decks necessary to remove the 19 kHz pilot tone from an FM signal that would otherwise make **Dolby NR** tracking difficult.

**NAB:** National Association of Broadcasters. A trade organization for radio and television broadcasting, which also sets some standards.

**Noise Reduction (NR):** The reduction of unwanted, spurious sound (such as hiss) from an audio signal.

**NTSC:** National Television Standards Committee. The group that set the U.S. standard for color television in 1953, NTSC now is shorthand for the outdated standard itself (and derisively referred to as Never Twice the Same Color), having 525 lines/frame of resolution and a frame-rate of 29.97.

**OEM:** Original Equipment Manufacturer.

**OFC:** Oxygen Free Copper.

**Ogg Vorbis:** An open source, royalty-free audio **Compression** format sponsored by Xiph.org, it is generally considered to be audibly superior to most other **Compression** schemes, especially **MP3**.

**Op-Amp:** Operational Amplifier. A low-power differential amplifier, suitable for line, phono cartridge, and microphone-level signal voltages. Its characteristics include high **Gain**, high input impedance, low output impedance, and wide bandwidth.

**Oversampling:** When converting analog to digital (or digital to analog) audio data, processing at a sampling frequency at least twice as great as the original.

**P-Mount:** A kind of cartridge (sometimes referred to as T4P) with four solid terminals that attach to the end of a tonearm, generally with little or no adjustment.

**PAL:** Phase Alternating Line. The television standard for most of the world (that is not **NTSC** or **SECAM**), it has 625 lines/frame of resolution and a frame rate of 25.

**PASC:** Precision Adaptive Sub-band Coding. A lossy **Compression** scheme developed Philips.

**PCM:** Pulse-Code Modulation. The most common form of digitally encoding an audio signal.

**PDA:** Personal Digital Assistant. A handheld device originally with limited memory meant to store an individual's calendar, to-do list, address book, etc., but which now can incorporate audio, video, and wireless functionality, including Web browsing.

**Péritel:** *See SCART.*

**PLL:** Phase Locked Loop. A servo mechanism used to ensure a constant speed. They are found in Direct Drive turntables, capstan motors of tape decks, and are also used in digital audio input receivers to reduce clock **Jitter** errors.

**PMC:** Personal Media Center.

**PMP:** Personal Media Player.

**Point Source:** A speaker that radiates sound only towards the front and from a single point. *See also Dipole.*

**PPCM:** Packed PCM (*see MLP*).

**Progressive Scan:** The opposite of interlaced, a method of displaying video images in which every horizontal line is drawn on screen in a single pass one after the other to create a complete frame or single full-screen video image, resulting in a brighter and more stable picture.

**PVP:** Personal Video Player.

**PWM:** Pulse Width Modulation. One method of digitally encoding an audio signal.

**Quantization:** The process of converting digital to analog, or vice versa.

**Quantization Noise:** When quantization is done in the audible range, it introduces quantization noise into the signal, which is why most **CD** players "oversample" (sampling at a frequency out of the audible range) the digital signal.

**RFI:** Radio Frequency Interference.

**RIAA:** Recording Industry Association of America, a trade group for the recording industry.

**RIAA Equalization:** The standardized equalization curve for modern phono playback.

**SACD:** Super Audio Compact Disc. A rival high-resolution disc format to **DVD-A**, having many of the same benefits, developed by Philips and Sony, using **DSD** encoding.

**RMS:** Abbreviation for Root Mean Square, a kind of power rating.

**RSPC:** Reed-Solomon Product Code. A very robust error correction scheme, applied to a large amount of data.

**Sampling Frequency (or Rate):** The number of times per second an analog signal (amplitude) is measured when being converted to digital.

**SAP:** Secure Audio Path. A piece of software built into Windows XP to thwart unauthorized media copying by encrypting data and using authenticated or "trusted" hardware (sound cards).

**SBM:** Super Bit Mapping. A digital filtering process developed by Sony that shapes **Quantization Noise** in an attempt to make a 16-bit resolution format (such as **CD**) sound like a 20-bit format by remapping 20- or 24-bit data streams to the 16-bit standard.

**SCART:** Syndicat des Constructeurs d'Appareils Radiorécepteurs et Téléviseurs. A 21-pin video connection found on European DVD players. In France it is often referred to as Péritel or Euroconnector.

**SCMS:** Serial Copy Management System (often pronounced "scams"). A copy-protection scheme that allows one digital recording from an original digital source, but not a further digital copy from that copy.

**SDDS:** Sony Dynamic Digital Sound. A seven-speaker **Surround Sound** format for commercial theaters, incompatible and therefore in competition with **Dolby** and **DTS**. There is no consumer version of SDDS.

**SECAM:** Sequential Couleur Avec Memoire, or Sequential Colour with Memory. This is the television standard in France and former French colonies, and uses the same frame rate and resolution as **PAL**, but transmits color sequentially. Also referred to as System Even Crappier than the American Method.

**Shibata stylus:** *See Hyper-Elliptical.*

**S/N (or SNR):** Signal-to-Noise Ratio. The maximum signal of a device compared to the amplitude of its background noise, measured in decibels.

**Sorbothane:** A polyurethane material that absorbs energy.

**S/PDIF:** Sony/Philips Digital Interface Format. A standardized protocol (IEC958) for transmitting digital audio signals between consumer-grade products. S/PDIF differs most importantly from the professional grade **AES/EBU** protocol in that the former carries the **SCMS** and the latter carries subcode information to identify source and destination. S/PDIF does not refer to a particular kind of connection or interface, although it is sometimes erroneously labeled as such on some products.

**SPL:** Abbreviation for Sound Pressure Levell.

**SR-D:** Spectral Recording Digital. *See Dolby Digital.*

**Stereo:** The two-**Channel** reproduction of audio information from which our ears can derive directional and spatial information about the recording site, rendering (when done right) a three-dimensional image in front of the listener. This term also can stand for the general labeling of the equipment used for home music reproduction.

**Stereohedron Stylus.** *See Hyper-Elliptical.*

**ST-Type Interface:** An optical method of sending **S/PDIF**-encoded digital information from one component to another.

**Stylus:** The part of a phono cartridge that is in direct contact with the record and traces the groove.

**Subwoofer:** Most often found in a home theater setup (but not unheard of in an audio-only playback system), the subwoofer reproduces the very lowest frequencies.

**Surround Sound:** The use of three or more **Channels** that seeks to give the listener a more realistic theater experience in the home. Usually this requires several speakers, set up not only in front of the viewer/listener but in back of them as well. The goal is not only to produce a three-dimensional image in front of the listener/viewer (*see Stereo*), but 360° around. *See also 5.1/6.1, Dolby, Stereo, THX.*

**S-Video:** A common video connection that separates a signal's color information and brightness for a superior picture (compared to **Composite**).

**S-VHS:** Super-VHS. A format developed by JVC that offers 400 lines of vertical resolution, compared to **VHS**'s 250. Although the size of the cassette is identical to **VHS**, the two formats are incompatible.

**Sweet Spot:** The position (in relationship to loudspeakers) where a listener can "lock in" on the best stereophonic effect. The farther away from this spot the listener goes (left, right, front, or back) the poorer the perceived sound reproduction.

**THD:** Total Harmonic Distortion. A measurement of the distortion produced by the total of all the harmonics (multiples of a given frequency not meant to be reproduced), expressed as a percentage of the strength of the fundamental.

**THX:** Not a multi-channel format, as it is often misunderstood to be, THX refers to a certifiable standard of sound reproduction that equipment so labeled meets. A THX-certified piece of equipment (or movie theater, or even home theater) meets all of the requirements that THX engineers have set in place to ensure a consistent level of playback from unit to unit (or theater to theater). THX is not an acronym, but is named after George Lucas's first movie, originally a student film and later turned into a full-length feature titled *THX 1138*.

**TIM:** Transient Intermodulation Distortion. **Distortion** that occurs in an amplifying stage with large amounts of inverse feedback and high frequency phase shift, when a strong incoming transient overloads the stage before the fed-back signal has time to attenuate the transient.

**TosLink:** Trademarked name (by Toshiba, generically known as "**EIA-J** optical") for a kind of connection that allows an optical cable to carry digital information to another piece of equipment. Sometimes erroneously referred to as a **S/PDIF** connection (which is the protocol of the data stream).

**Transducer:** Something that converts one form of energy into another form, for example, a speaker (which converts electrical energy into sound, or acoustic energy).

**Tweaking:** Fine-tuning.

**UAA:** Universal Audio Architecture. A Microsoft initiative to improve computer audio (and audio driver support). It is to be incorporated into the next Windows operating system, Longhorn.

**UHDV:** Ultra High Definition Video. May replace **HDTV**.

**Unbalanced Connection:** *See Balanced.*

**Van den Hul Stylus:** *See Line Contact.*

**VBR:** Variable Bit Rate. An **MP3 Compression** scheme that varies the data **Compression** according to the amount of data produced at any given moment, with a goal of higher quality sound and smaller file sizes.

**VCR:** Videocassette Recorder.

**Vented Loudspeaker:** A ported speaker cabinet that allows the acoustic energy created by the rearward motion of a **Driver** to escape the enclosure.

**VHS:** Vertical Helix Scan. A videocassette format developed by JVC to compete with Sony's Betamax cassette.

**VTA:** Vertical Tracking Angle. The angle between the surface plane of a record and an imaginary line between the **Stylus** and the cantilever pivot.

**W:** Abbreviation for watt.

**XLR:** Standard three-pin connector for balanced interconnects.

Adams, John J. *Complete Guide to Audio.* Indianapolis, IN: Howard W. Sams, 1998.

*Application Guide for Isolated Ground Wiring Devices* (NEMA Standards Publication), 2002, <www.nema.org/DocUploads/059B3D05-172A-4652-A31E0F91F36C1EB/AppGuide_IsoGrnd.pdf> (June 5, 2003).

*Audio Systems Technology: Handbook for Installers & Engineers, Levels I, II, and III.* Cedar Rapids, IA: National Systems Contractors Association, 2000.

Benade, Arthur H. *Fundamentals of Musical Acoustics.* New York: Oxford University Press, 1976.

Borwick, John, ed. *Loudspeaker and Headphone Handbook.* 3rd ed. Oxford: Focal Press, 2001.

Brain, Marshall. "How CDs Work." n.d. <electronics.howstuffworks.com/cd.htm> (January 5, 2004).

Cameron, Derek. *Audio Technology Systems: Principles, Applications, and Troubleshooting.* Reston, VA: Reston Publishing, 1978.

Cohen, Alan A. *Audio Technology Fundamentals.* Indianapolis, IN: Howard W. Sams, 1989.

Davis, Mark F. "What's Really Important in Loudspeaker Performance?" *High Fidelity* (June 1978): 53-57.

Elliott, Rod. *The Audio Pages: Audio Articles.* June 9, 2001. <sound.westhost.com/articles.htm> (July 10, 2003).

*Encyclopedia of Recorded Sound in the United States*, edited by Guy A. Marco. New York: Garland, 1993.

Ferstler, Howard. *High Fidelity Audio/Video Systems: A Critical Guide for Owners.* Jefferson, NC: McFarland, 1991.

Galo, Gary. "Loudspeakers: A Short History." *Speaker Builder* (June 1994): 18-21, 64; (July 1994): 30-31, 34, 38-41.

Harley, Robert. *The Complete Guide to High-End Audio.* 2nd ed. Albuquerque, NM: Acapella, 1998.

Hill, Brad. *The Digital Songstream: Mastering the World of Digital Music.* New York: Routledge, 2003.

Holt, J. Gordon. *The Audio Glossary.* Peterborough, NH: Audio Amateur Press, 1990.

Jayne, Allan W., Jr. *Television and Video Advice.* 2002. <members.aol.com/ajaynejr/video.htm> (June 10, 2004).

Kobel, Alen. "HDMI—One Year Later: A New Standard for Transmitting Digital Video Signals." *Widescreen Review*, Issue 24, May 2004. <www.hdmi.org/pdf/WSR04HDMI.pdf> (June 10, 2004).

*LabGuy's World: The History of Video Tape Recorders before Betamax and VHS*. November 25, 2002. <www.labguysworld.com/> (January 9, 2003).

Maes, Jan, and Marc Vercammen, eds. *Digital Audio Technology: A Guide to CD, MiniDisc, SACD, DVD(A), MP3 and DAT*. 4th ed. Oxford: Focal Press, 2001.

Media Sciences. *CD and DVD Glossary*. n.d. <www.mscience.com/gloss.html> (January 7, 2003).

*Planning and Caring for Library Audio Facilities*, edited by James P. Cassaro, MLA Technical Report no. 17. Canton, MA: Music Library Association, 1989.

Pohlmann, Ken C. *The Compact Disc Handbook*. 2nd ed. The Computer Music and Digital Audio Series, 5. Madison, WI: A-R Editions, 1992.

———. *Principles of Digital Audio*. 4th ed. New York: McGraw-Hill, 2000. <www.netLibrary.com/urlapi.asp?action=summary&v=1&bookid=5232> (January 21, 2004).

Quilter, Patrick H. "The Story Behind the Specs: How to Compare Amplifier Power Ratings." *Christian Sound & Song*, no. 4, n.d. <www.soundandsong.com/Issue004/004_PowerAmpRatings.html> (October 31, 2003).

Sharpless, Graham. *New Formats for Music: DVD & SACD*. Deluxe Global Media Services, 2001-03. July 30, 2003. <www.disctronics.co.uk/downloads/tech_docs/dvdaudio.pdf> (March 1, 2004).

Sinclair, Ian R., ed. *Audio and Hi-Fi Handbook*. Rev. 3rd ed. Oxford: Newnes, 2000.

Streicher, Ron, and F. Alton Everest. *The New Stereo Soundbook*. 2nd ed. Pasadena, CA: Audio Engineering Associates, 1998.

Taylor, Jim. *DVD Frequently Asked Questions (And Answers)*. January 4, 2003. <www.dvddemystified.com/dvdfaq.html> (January 22, 2003).

Utz, Peter. *Introduction to Audio*. The Computer Music and Digital Audio Series, 20. Middleton, WI: A-R Editions, 2003.

White, Glenn D. *The Audio Dictionary*. 2nd ed. Seattle: University of Washington Press, 1991. (Also available as a CD-ROM.)

# SOURCES FOR EQUIPMENT REVIEWS

In the text of this book I revealed my skepticism of most reviews of audio and video equipment. Nevertheless there are a number of journals and websites devoted to the topic, and below is a list. At the very least, perusing them will keep you up-to-date on the latest trends and innovations.

*The Absolute Sound*
(www.theabsolutesound.com)

*AudioAsylum*
(www.audioasylum.com)

*The Audiophile Voice*
(www.audiophilevoice.com)

AudioREVIEW.com
(www.audioreview.com)

*audioXpress Magazine*
(www.audioXpress.com)

C|NET
(www.cnet.com)

eCoustics.com
(www.ecoustics.com)

*Enjoy the Music.com Review Magazine*
(www.enjoythemusic.com/magazine)

*Fi: The Magazine of Music and Sound*

*Gramophone*
(www.gramophone.co.uk)

*Hi-Fi Choice*
(www.hifichoice.co.uk)

*Hi-Fi News*
(www.hifinews.co.uk)

*High Fidelity Review*
(HighFidelityReview.com)

*The Perfect Vision*
(www.theperfectvision.com)

*The $ensible Sound*
(www.sensiblesound.com)

*Sound and Vision*
(soundandvisionmag.com)

*Stereophile*
(www.stereophile.com)

*Widescreen Review*
(www.widescreenreview.com)

## About the Author

---

**Jim Farrington** is head of public services at the Sibley Music Library, Eastman School of Music, Rochester, New York, where he also teaches music bibliography and a seminar on the history and aesthetics of sound recordings. He formerly held the position of music librarian and director of the World Music Archives at Wesleyan University. He has served on the board of directors for the Music Library Association and as editor of the *MLA Newsletter*. He recently finished a term as president of the Association for Recorded Sound Collections.